WRITING MATTERS

Peter G. Beidler

Second Edition

coffeetownpress

Seattle Washington

This book was set in Century Schoolbook and Courier New fonts.
Printed and bound by Amazon.com.

Copyright © 2013 by Coffeetown Press, Seattle, Washington.
Contact: info@coffeetownpress.com
Second edition

ISBN: 978-1-60381-174-3 (Trade Paper)
ISBN: 978-1-60381-175-0 (eBook)

Printed in the United States of America.

Library of Congress Control Number: 2013935064

Library of Congress Cataloging-in-Publication Data
Beidler, Peter G.
        Writing matter/s / Peter G. Beidler
        Includes index.
        ISBN: 978-1-60381-174-3 (Trade Paper)
        ISBN: 978-1-60381-175-0
        1. English Language—Rhetoric.   I. Title
        PE1408.B4693   2009
        808'.042—dc22   2009022133

CONTENTS

About the Author

Peter G. Beidler is the Lucy G. Moses Professor of English emeritus at Lehigh University. He has published widely on medieval literature, American literature, American Indian literature, and teaching. In 1983 he was named national Professor of the Year by the Council for Advancement and Support of Education in Washington, D.C. He spent the 1987–1988 academic year as a Fulbright professor at Sichuan University in Chengdu, China. In 1995–1996 he was a visiting professor at Baylor University in Waco, Texas. He is now retired and living in Seattle, Washington.

About the Second Edition

The twenty-six basic chapters have been so well received that I have made only a few small changes in them for this second edition. I have, however, added four student-written essays for discussion and expanded the section on EDITING MATTERS.

PREFACE

This little book is designed to help college students
learn to write better essays. In its earliest draft it was
a simple set of mimeographed guidelines for my first-
year students who seemed to learn better by seeing my
mini-lectures than by hearing them. Although many of
my examples are drawn from courses in which students
write about their own lives and their reactions to college
life, the principles of good writing that I discuss will
apply to almost any courses in which students are
expected to write argumentative essays.

This book is designed to teach itself. Each chapter
is not only a self-contained lesson on some feature
of writing, but is also a model of the kind of writing
that students are expected to do in college. It has an
introduction, a thesis or central argument supported by
evidence or examples, transitions, and a conclusion.

In addition to designing *Writing Matters* for use
in courses that require systematic writing, I have
also designed it with a view to the kind of writing
that professional men and women will do after they
leave college. Not only do I include an early chapter

specifically on "Writing in the Professional World," but the principles of good writing that I emphasize throughout the book will apply to such writing: the need to see most writing tasks as an argument for a specific view, the need for concrete evidence in support of that view, the need for clarity, and the need for an appropriate written "voice." The brief final section on editing gives helpful hints that will prove useful for writers at all levels.

Some writing textbooks move from a discussion of sentences to a discussion of paragraphs and finally to a discussion of the whole essay. *Writing Matters* takes the opposite approach, beginning with the whole essay (see, for example, Chapter 3). I have found that most students learn to write better if they are asked to write full essays right off. Doing so gives them an argumentative context within which to polish their individual sentences and paragraphs. The chapters, however, are designed to be independent units, and teachers can assign the various chapters in any order they find convenient for their own classrooms.

I am grateful to the many students and colleagues who have helped me to develop this approach to teaching writing, particularly Lucy Bednar, Rob Dornsife, Kathleen Mayberry, Susan Haytmanek, and James Wallace. I am grateful to Gene Mater for his brilliant drawings. I owe special thanks to my former student, my collaborator, and my friend Marion Egge, who worked with me during the various stages of production to give *Writing Matters* its current shape and to make this book happen.

To the Student

When I began my teaching career at Lehigh University I had no idea how to teach writing. I knew something about how to write, because I had, after all, majored in English and had written lots of papers. But how in the world would I teach writing? In my first decade or so of teaching writing I learned a few tricks that made me sound like a teacher of writing some of the time, but I was still mostly confused and mystified and full of questions about how to teach writing. Finally I decided to try to be somewhat more systematic in my questioning. I asked myself three questions: How do I write? How did I learn to write that way? How can I teach in such a way that others can learn as I did?

How do I write? Well, of course, that depends on what I am writing. In a letter to my daughter I write one way. In a letter to my insurance company I write another way. In a newspaper article. . . . In a committee report. . . . In a short story. . . . In a poem. . . . I decided that in answering my question about how I write I had to focus on argumentative writing, the kind of writing I had done as a college student. I read a few of my early papers and noticed certain common features. Each

contained, for example, an introductory paragraph
in which I stated my main idea. Each contained
paragraphs in which I offered support for my main idea.
Each contained transitional words and phrases that
showed the connections between my various supporting
paragraphs. There was nothing great about any of those
papers, but in them I had found a way to express myself
on subjects I had grown to care about. More important,
I discovered that I still, in most of my professional
writing, write essays that have most of those same
features.

Having described how I wrote, I was ready for
the question: How did I learn to write that way? I
really was not sure. Certainly, I did not remember
having been taught to write. I remember being taught
something about dependent clauses in high school,
but learning grammar is not learning writing. As for
college, I had skipped the writing courses Earlham
College offered and took instead courses like "Freshman
Humanities" and "The Development of the Novel." My
teachers sometimes criticized my writing and gave me
suggestions, especially about the content of my papers,
but they spent little time actively teaching writing. I
decided that I must have learned to write mostly by
reading. I had always read for fun. It occurs to me now
that perhaps I learned to write-through-reading in the
same way that many students in other countries learn
to speak-through-listening. I discovered that some of my
best students the year I taught in China had learned to
speak by listening to the Voice of America or to other
English-language radio programs. They had trained

their tongues by noticing how good speakers talked. I must, similarly, have trained my pen by noticing how good writers wrote.

Having discovered a bit about how I wrote and having developed some notions about how I had learned, I was ready for the toughest question of all: How could I help my students learn to write as I had learned to write? It seemed impossible. My students, after all, had been raised watching television, not reading books. Still, maybe I could find a textbook that would give my students helpful models of good argumentative writing along with helpful commentary about what made them good. I tried, but in the end, I gave up the search and decided to write a few little essays that would do for my students what I thought needed to be done. I photocopied enough copies for my students and distributed them. My essays were about argumentative writing, but they were also models of the kind of writing that I thought would help beginning college writers. The next year, having noticed what I thought was an improvement in my students' writing, I wrote a few more essays. The year after that I wrote a few more. Before long it seemed sensible to put these free-floating essays into photocopied booklets. Soon those booklets evolved into this printed version, *Writing Matters*.

This book was born, then, because I did not know how to teach writing.

CHAPTER 1

WRITING IN THE PROFESSIONAL WORLD

You do not need a course in writing. After all, you have been taking English courses ever since you were seven. Because you are planning to major in engineering or accounting or computer science or biology, you will not need to know how to write anyhow. To succeed in that big world out there on the other side of graduation, all you will need are a telephone, a computer, a conference call, and a good secretary who will do your writing for you. You will do the creative thinking. Besides, you know that writing is not very important anyhow and that you will spend almost none of your time on the job doing the mundane tasks of writing. Right? Sorry. But do not take my word for it. Let me tell you what people who know the real world of professional work say about the most neglected skill in business, about the importance of writing in the professions, about the amount of time professional people spend doing writing in their jobs, and about writing skills in high-tech corporations.

Well, what is the most neglected skill in business? In 1983 the *Los Angeles Times* reported the results of a nationwide survey of over two hundred business executives by Communispond, Inc., a communications research group. The survey asked these executives just that question. The answers were impressive. A full 80% of the executives surveyed listed writing as the most neglected skill in business—not accounting or technological literacy or electronics, but good old-fashioned writing. Why do so many executives think writing is a neglected skill? Surely it is in part because bad writing costs money. Another study revealed that bad writing costs American business an estimated one billion dollars a year in wasted time, lost contracts, and alienated customers (*Business Digest*, November 1984, p. 47).

If writing is the most neglected skill in business, how important do professional people think writing is for corporate executives? In 1984 Hodge-Cronin, a Chicago-based management consulting firm, conducted a survey of over eight hundred chief executive officers (CEOs) in many fields—insurance, manufacturing, banking, technology, utilities, and so on. Their survey showed that 98% of the responding CEOs said that writing was important for success in their own and other executive positions. More than 83% felt that their younger executives were not well trained in writing. At the end of the Hodge-Cronin report was the suggestion that companies trying to recruit top executive talent should ask the candidates to write several paragraphs on how they understand the position they are being considered for, how they would fit into the organization, their management philosophy, and the like. Doing so, the report suggested, would help the companies not only to understand the views of the person being considered for the position but would help them to discover whether the applicant could write clearly and concisely.

If businesspeople know that writing is the most neglected skill in business, and if professional people know how important writing is to their success, just how much time do college-educated professionals spend at writing in their jobs? One study showed that most college-educated professionals spend at least 30% of their time on the job doing writing-related tasks: planning, organizing, drafting, and revising. In an average week they write three internal memos or emails, five letters outside the company, and two business or technical reports (*College English,* October 1982, pp. 557–69). A 1990 Communispond survey of over three hundred business executives at the rank of vice president and above revealed that three-quarters of them wrote more than ten letters, reports, and other business documents per week. "But I am going to be an engineer," you may say. "Indeed, I decided to major in engineering so that I would not have to write. I am a numbers person, a diagram person, a machine person, a computer person. As an engineer I will not have to write." Sorry. That is not the way the world of engineering works. Separate studies conducted by

the Massachusetts Institute of Technology and the
University of Wisconsin showed that engineers spend,
on the average, at least 25% of their time on the job
doing writing tasks (*Graduating Engineer*, March 1984,
pp. 25–28).

So much for business and engineering. What about
the brave new world of high tech? Surely professionals
in high technology can escape the need to write. Sorry.
Not long ago mathematics professor Sharon K. Hauge
interviewed thirty corporate executives in high-tech
corporations in the Washington, D.C., metropolitan
area. She reported that all of the executives she
interviewed "stressed the importance of having excellent
oral and written communication skills":

> These skills included the ability to listen, to
> write technical reports, to formulate problems in
> precise language, to communicate recommendations
> in a convincing way . . . to give instructions, to
> ask the right questions. . . . Everyone who was
> interviewed indicated that poor communication
> skills, particularly written communication skills,
> were the most common problem of new employees
> in their corporations. ("Skills for the New World,"
> *College Teaching,* 34, Fall 1986, 142)

I know what u r thinking—that my examples come
from way back in the 1980s, b4 u were even born, and
that in these modern twenty-first century times of
emailing, thumbing instant messages, and twittering,
do I really need 2 write anymore? OK, I c what u mean.
Here are some more recent examples:

The Writing section [of the Scholastic Aptitude Test], which we introduced in 2005, has emerged as the most predictive part of the SAT in terms of measuring the potential for college success. Furthermore, we see this predictive value in students from all racial and ethnic groups. The introduction of the Writing section has also encouraged high schools to place more emphasis on writing, which helps give students the skills they need to succeed in college. (Gaston Caperton, president of the College Board and former two-term governor of West Virginia, in a speech given August 26, 2008)

A survey of 120 major American corporations employing nearly 8 million people concludes that in today's workplace writing is a "threshold skill" for hiring and promotion among salaried (i.e., professional) employees. Survey results indicate that writing is a ticket to professional opportunity, while poorly written job applications are a figurative kiss of death. Estimates based on the survey returns reveal that employers spend billions annually correcting writing deficiencies. . . . In a nutshell, the survey confirms our conviction that individual opportunity in the United States depends critically on the ability to present one's thoughts coherently, cogently, and persuasively on paper. (The National Commission on Writing, *Writing: A Ticket to Work . . . or a Ticket Out*, published September 2004, pp. 3, 5)

In the business world, your writing may be your first and only chance to impress someone you want to work with. I've seen far too many letters,

resumes, and proposals that disqualify the writer
by sloppy construction and grammatical errors.
Strong, clear writing is assumed to demonstrate
clarity of thinking, an essential asset in today's
business world. (Charlie Liekweg, 2012, recently
retired President and CEO of AAA Washington
and former Vice President, Operations, GTE
Corporation)

But you already know how important writing is. In
a 2008 study called *Writing, Technology, and Teens*,
Amanda Lenhart and her colleagues report on the basis
of an extensive survey that "Teens write a lot, but they
do not think of their e-mails, instant and text messages
as writing." Indeed, we seem to have invented a new
word, "texting" to distinguish these informal electronic
messages from "writing," which is a more serious and
sustained endeavor. Lenhart goes on to say, "This
disconnect matters because teens believe good writing
is an essential skill for success and that more writing
instruction at school would help them." Indeed it would.

During an informal question-and-answer session
following his stump speech in Fairfax, Virginia, on July
10, 2008, Barack Obama, then running for president the
first time, spoke of the importance of being able to write
so as to "give voice to our opinions in a coherent way."
He went on to say that, "just as a financial matter, in
terms of getting a job, knowing how to write is a good
thing. . . . These days the kids all know how to text
message, using a *u* for *you* and all these symbols I don't
understand. But when you are applying for a job you
will not be asked if you can text a message. They'll be

asking you if you can write a letter or a memorandum and communicate in proper English with others." It seems that everyone agrees that writing matters. So if you want to be president, or just want a job, read on.

CHAPTER 2

NERVOUS GRUMBLINGS ABOUT WRITING

Many beginning writers think that good writing is a special, almost magical, art. On the contrary, good writing is something that all of you can do right now. As someone who taught writing for forty years, I heard over and over again the nervous grumblings of beginning writers who had somehow become convinced that they could not write and who therefore did not like to try. Here are four of the most common of these nervous grumblings.

The first nervous grumbling is, "I just can't write. I've been taking English for years, and I even got good grades a few times, but writing is still a mystery. Some people are born knowing how to write, but I was born untalented, I guess." Nonsense. To be sure, some people write with greater grace and ease than others, but not because they were born that way. The chances are that

they write with grace and ease now in part because
their parents read to them when they were very young
and in part because as they grew up they spent many
hours reading. Just as it is easier to learn French at a
young age when surrounded by French-speaking people,
so it is easier to learn to write if, at a young age, we
read, and read, and read. Still, many men and women
have learned French by studying it in college, and a
far greater number of men and women have learned
to write good, solid English prose in college. With hard
work, concentration, and receptivity to criticism, you
can learn to be a good writer. You will discover, of
course, that when you have something that you *want* to
write about, something you *need* to communicate to a
real audience, you will automatically be a better writer
than if you are writing exercises and examples just to
fill an academic course requirement. Within the context
of a college course, however, you can learn the basics of
effective writing.

The second nervous grumbling is, "I don't have a big
enough vocabulary to write well." Nonsense. You have a
big enough vocabulary to read the daily newspaper and
college-level math, science, and history textbooks. If you
did not, you would never have been admitted to college
in the first place. If your vocabulary is big enough for
those activities, it is big enough for you to write well.
Good writing does not depend on a big vocabulary.
Indeed, a vocabulary that is *too* big can be a greater
impediment to effective communication than one that
is too small. Clear communication is often impeded by
big words, because by using such words you run the

NONSENSE! YOU CAN LEARN TO BE A GOOD WRITER!

risk that your audience will not know what the words mean. The amazing thing about your vocabulary is that it develops along with you. As you expand your interests to include subjects requiring a larger vocabulary, you automatically develop the vocabulary to communicate about those subjects. If your Uncle Harry gave you a thesaurus for a high school graduation present so you could use it in college, I advise you to throw it away.

It will only get you into trouble. You already know the words you need to write well what *you* have to say.

The third nervous grumbling is, "I just can't seem to figure out what the teacher wants me to say in these essays." Nonsense. Your teachers do not much care what you say, if by that you mean what opinions you have. Your teachers will not criticize your writing because they disagree with your ideas. Your teachers do not care what you say about American politics, or whether you approve of your college's dining service, or how you feel about the morality of stem cell research. That is your business. Your teachers care about what you say only to the extent that it has bearing on how you make a case for what you believe. If you think college admissions officers are trying to deceive innocent high school students, your teachers will care about how well you support that view with evidence, examples, and logic, how well you have structured your paragraphs, whether you develop your point consistently, whether your sentences convey your ideas clearly. Your teachers will be more enthusiastic about a well-constructed essay that makes a point they disagree with than about a badly constructed essay that reflects their own opinions. In short, your teachers want you to say what you want to say; what they care most about is that you say it well.

The fourth nervous grumbling is, "I just can't think of anything to say about any of those topics." Nonsense. If you have lived and observed and thought for any of the years you have been alive, and if you have read the materials that your teacher has assigned to you, then you will be able to think of something to say. If you

cannot, you must be dead, in which case writing will
not matter much to you. It really does not take much to
think of something to say about a topic. If you are asked
to write an essay about your residence hall, for example,
you might consider arguing that the aging rat barn
should be torn down. You might consider arguing that
its peaceful atmosphere reminds you of your own home
back in Cherry Hill. You might argue that residence
hall living has many advantages over fraternity or
sorority living. Or that coed residence halls are an
invasion of privacy. Or that some university students
are discriminated against in your residence hall. Or that
colleges should save money by having students perform
many of the maintenance services now performed by
professional cleaning staff. And so on. Any of those
ideas about your residence hall could be developed into
a fine essay. There is no end to what you might write
about such a topic if you think and if you trust your own
opinions.

Of course you can write. There is no special magic to
it. You do not have to be an English or journalism major
to do it. The nervous grumbling that I have not heard
very often is this: "I can't write because I don't believe in
myself." That fifth complaint might not be nonsense.

CHAPTER 3

WHAT IS AN
ACCEPTABLE ESSAY?

No one expects you to write prizewinning essays in a
college writing course. Some of you will if you work
hard and believe in yourselves, but you do not have
to do brilliant writing to succeed in such a course. To
succeed, however, you must write acceptable essays. To
write one of those you must, of course, have something
of substance to say, and you must use proper grammar
and decently constructed sentences. Beyond that,
however, *an acceptable essay is a bold, clear, and well-
developed argument presented in a unified, cohesive, and
organized form.* It is as simple as that. If your essays
do not get the same rave comments as those of your
classmates, it will probably be because your work does
not fully meet the standards set forth in that definition.
There are eighteen words in the italicized portion of

that sentence, but only six of them are important in
the present context. The standards for acceptability
fall generally into two groups of three each. The first
group has to do primarily with the content or subject
matter of the argument, while the second group has to
do primarily with the form, or arrangement, of it. Let us
consider the subject matter of the argument first.

An acceptable essay should be *bold*. Try to find
something unusual to say that will arouse the interest of
the readers of your essay: a new twist on how to get rid
of a blind date, a fresh statement about how educational
TV is a waste of time, your own special interpretation
of the Bill of Rights as it applies to life in a campus
residence hall, what it is like being the only woman on
a physics lab team, or whatever. An important part of
what I mean here is that you should *say* something.
Take a stand. Stand up in your essay and shout, "This
is what I believe." Do you or do you not think colleges
should offer no-need football scholarships? Get off the
fence. Do not say, "Well, maybe they should, but, then
again, maybe they shouldn't. There are advantages
either way." Of course there are, but your job is to argue
for one or the other. If you cannot, then pick another
topic. Be firm and definite. Your readers will tend not
to be much interested in a fainthearted, wishy-washy
essay. Convey self-assurance and conviction.

In addition to being bold, an acceptable essay must
be *clear*. If your readers must reread your essay, or a
part of it, to figure out what you are saying, then you
have failed. Your job as a writer is to make a reader's
job easy, to make your meaning so absolutely and

infallibly clear that everyone understands what you are saying. I have found that beginning writers are frequently surprised when they are told that their meaning in an essay is not clear. They tend to think the fault lies with the readers, not themselves. Almost invariably the opposite is true. The discrepancy lies in the fact that the writers know what is in their minds, whereas the readers know only what is on the paper. There are various causes for lack of clarity: failure to state a clear or specific main point; failure to repeat or emphasize it; failure to use specific examples; failure to use direct language. The most common cause of lack of clarity, however, is that writers miscalculate what their readers know. They think that because they know or believe something, of course their readers know or believe the same thing. Writers, therefore, fail to raise certain arguments or to explain certain situations, but just charge on, not realizing that they have left their readers in bewilderment back at the last crossroads. All writers have to learn, then, to base their writing not on what they, the writers, know, but on what their readers know.

Besides being bold and clear, an acceptable essay must present a *well-developed* argument. You must select and present supporting evidence in such a way that your readers are convinced by what you say. There are various kinds of argument: you may want to inspire your readers to do something; or to see something from a different point of view; or to understand something; or to feel something not felt before. Whatever your purpose in writing the essay, you need support for your argument. For example, if you want to argue that solar heat is not practical, you may want to develop that idea with a story about your neighbor who installed it last summer only to find that it will take him seventeen years to save enough in fuel bills to pay for the system, and then only if his solar system needs no maintenance in that seventeen-year period. Of course, if you do use this example to develop your point, be sure to relate it to the main point in your essay by stating the connection: "Therefore, solar heating costs too much to be practical." If you do not develop your ideas sufficiently, your audience will not be convinced, and you will have failed.

Most of my discussion so far has been about the subject of your essay: what you must say to make your argument bold, clear, and developed enough to be convincing. The rest of my discussion deals more with the form of your essay, because how you say what is bold, clear, and well developed is obviously important also. To be fully acceptable, your argument must be unified, cohesive, and organized.

An acceptable essay must be *unified*. It must make one clearly identifiable point. The best way to ensure unity is to write a strong thesis sentence, and then to make sure that everything else you write in the essay somehow develops that thesis sentence. The thesis sentence—a capsule summary of your main point—is so important that I devote my next chapter to a discussion of how to write the kind of thesis sentence that will help you most as you write your essay. Do not be surprised if, in a conference concerning an essay you wrote about how hateful your roommate is, your instructor asks you to explain why you have a sentence in your third paragraph on your roommate's dislike of hot dogs and sauerkraut. That information probably has nothing to do with his hatefulness. If it does, your instructor will insist that you show why not liking hot dogs and sauerkraut makes your roommate hateful. Without unity, an essay falls apart.

In addition to being unified, an acceptable essay must be *cohesive*. Its parts must stick together. Cohesion is obviously closely related to unity. Unless the essay sticks together there will be—or will appear to be—no unity. Cohesion, however, is really a matter of connectives, of the glue or the strings that hold together the different parts of an essay. We sometimes use the word "transitions" to refer to the connective devices by which writers announce that they are finished with one part of an argument and going on to the next part. We sometimes use the word "signposts" to refer to the quite explicit information that writers give to their readers about where they are in the development of their support for their thesis. Whatever the terminology we use to explain cohesion, your readers will appreciate your telling them, quite directly, where you are and where you are going. Words or phrases like "next," "on the other hand," and "another example" help. Even more helpful are more extended signposts like, "Having considered how the community college prepares older students for professional jobs, let us consider now how it prepares them for continued study in four-year colleges." The best place for these transitions or signposts is at the start of your paragraphs, because it is there that

readers who initially like to skim a paper will look for
evidence of the overall structure of your paper. In a
longer essay, cohesion usually also involves connective
sentences or paragraphs explaining the relationships
between the larger sections of your paper.

Finally, an acceptable essay must be *organized*.
Some principle of arrangement must be made evident to
your readers. If your readers are to know where they are
at any given point in your argument, they must be given
a clear notion of how you are structuring your essay.
The structure of your essay, the organizational principle
of it, can be shown by means of an outline, or skeleton
sketch:

> A. Subject matter of argument
>   1. Bold
>   2. Clear
>   3. Developed
> B. Form of argument
>   1. Unified
>   2. Cohesive
>   3. Organized.

Normally writers do not give such a sketch. Rather,
they make the structural principle of the essay so clear
that readers can construct their own mental outline.
My introductory paragraph in the chapter you are now
reading, along with the introductory sentences in each
of the other paragraphs, is an attempt to direct your
attention to that structural principle. In a later chapter
I discuss several kinds of organizational structures most
frequently useful in college writing. For now, I want
merely to emphasize that there are various ways of

organizing essays. Your job as writer is first to choose the organizing principle that best presents and supports your argument and then to make sure that your readers know that that is the organizing principle you have chosen. Unless the skeleton is strong, the essay looks like a formless blob.

It does not take much to write an acceptable essay, but it does take these six features. If your essays are substantial, if they are mechanically clean, and if they demonstrate that you can write bold, clear, and well-developed arguments that are unified, cohesive, and organized, you will find that your essays are quite acceptable.

CHAPTER 4

YOUR THESIS SENTENCE

Good writing is fun, rewarding, and ego-satisfying, but very few good writers can tell you truthfully that it is easy. Like anything else worth doing, writing takes time, dedication, and hard work. There are ways, however, to make it easier. Do your reading assignments. Listen to your instructor's advice. When you get the topics for your essay, start immediately doing what is sometimes called "invention" or "brainstorming." Let your mind range over the topic you have selected. Jot down any ideas that pop into it. Explore the relationships among those ideas. Start focusing on what you know and how you feel about your topic. Keeping in mind that most college essays are extended arguments, or attempts to defend an opinion by persuading readers that a certain belief is valid, push around your ideas on these subjects. Do so until you begin to feel an opinion emerging, an argument that is distinctively yours and that you can imagine someone else disagreeing with. All of these steps make the actual writing of your essay, once you begin it, infinitely easier. If I could give you only one piece of advice about how to make your writing task easier, however, it would be this: take the time to compose a careful thesis sentence for your essay. By a "thesis sentence" I mean a one-sentence statement of your central argument in the paper, the key point you want to make. More needless work and wasted words have been generated among beginning writers by careless thesis sentences than by any other single cause. Let us examine some of the thesis sentences that you might use as the basis for an essay. If you do not come to see that some of these thesis sentences would make your job easier than others, well, it is your funeral.

"Funerals in America." Such a so-called statement is of little use to you because it is not a complete sentence. A thesis sentence must above all express a complete thought. Our first example may be a title or a topic, but it is not a sentence. It has no verb, no predicate. It cannot make your job easier because it does not say anything specific about your argument.

"I will write about funerals in America." Well, at least you have a sentence there, with a subject ("I") and a verb ("will write"), but the sentence takes the focus off your true subject (funerals) and puts it on the writer and the task of writing. More important, it tells nothing about what you will say about funerals. Besides, is not "funerals in America" too big a subject for an essay in a college writing course?

"I have been to five funerals this past year." Who
cares? And what *point* will you make about funerals?
That statement will not help you write the rest of
the essay, unless you plan to give a one-paragraph
narrative account of each funeral. Ho hum. But this
course is about argumentation, not narrative writing.
Drawing from your experience to make a point is one
thing. Writing about your experience for its own sake is
something quite different. Before you write your thesis,
mentally preface it with the phrase, "I believe that . . . ."
Your thesis should state an opinion, not a fact. Facts are
not arguable.

"I like going to funerals." Perhaps so, and
presumably you could list some of the reasons why
you like going to funerals: you like to see whether the
funeral director did a good job in making up the face,
you like to see the next of kin cry, you like . . . well,
whatever it is you do like about funerals. The trouble
with "I like . . ." theses, however, is that they are not
arguments. Never forget that an acceptable essay is,
by definition, an argument—an extended support for
an arguable opinion. If you like funerals, that is merely
a fact. If you like them, you like them. Period. No one
could argue that you do not like them. One of the tests
of a good thesis is to ask whether you could imagine
anyone seriously arguing against it. Another person
might not like going to funerals and might think you
were weird for liking them, but the question is one of
taste, not reason or argument.

"Funeral directors are nice." That thesis is too
general. How do you go about proving something about

niceness? Besides, it is absurd to say that *all* funeral directors are anything. Certainly you could not prove it. If you settle for such an opening, you are in for real trouble as you write your essay. You need a thesis sentence that focuses your efforts more closely.

"Funerals are sad, frightening, and depressing events." Perhaps you find them so, but notice that you have already violated the principle of *unity* by giving yourself three quite distinct theses to prove. And notice also that your list of three could be expanded indefinitely:

"Funerals are sad, frightening, depressing, expensive, intrusive, impersonal, exploitative, helpful. . . ." With a more focused thesis you know better when to quit because you know better what *one* point you must prove or support. Why not think further and select the one you have the most to say about or feel most strongly about, then begin marshaling the evidence that will help you to build a convincing argument? One of the biggest problems with most beginning theses is that they are too broad. They need to be limited or narrowed to something smaller. Often, indeed, this narrowing means focusing your thesis on a point that you had originally thought of as being merely a support for a much broader thesis. But do not forget to ask yourself whether you really believe your new thesis. Are you sure you find *funerals* depressing? Perhaps what you really mean is that you find *death* depressing.

"Funerals are helpful." Now you are getting warm, but you might improve on the "helpful." Most good thesis sentences focus on the predicate of the sentence, for it is usually the predicate that the writer will expand and say more about. Helpful to whom? Why? How? You need to do some more brainstorming here, nudging your ideas around to discover how funerals can help the living.

"Funerals help the bereaved come to terms with death." That is better. Then you can go on in the essay to show, specifically and with examples from your own experience or reading, just how funerals help the living come to terms with death. But are you sure you have all

that much to say about "coming to terms with death"—
whatever that means?

"Funerals help the living by giving them a chance
to understand the finality of death, to feel a sense of
comradeship with other mourners, and to reflect on
their own mortality." Fine! Now you have done it. The
thesis meets the "can-the-opposite-be-argued?" test
because it is quite reasonable to assume that someone
could argue that funerals are barbaric, capitalistic,
unnatural rituals designed not to help the living but to
exploit their feelings of guilt. Of course, this funerals-
help-the-living thesis is especially good because it is
more than a thesis. It goes beyond the simple statement
of your main argument and gives the organizational
pattern as well. With a thesis like this one, both you and
your reader know not merely what your destination is
but how you will get there. Getting there will be easy for
both of you.

Everyone knows that writing is a process. No
thoughtful writer simply sits down, starts at the
beginning, and plunges through to a triumphant ending.
Writing involves inventing and thinking and discovering
and experimenting and making false starts and turning
back and abandoning dead-end alleys. In arriving at a
workable thesis many good writers go through just the
kind of process implicit in this essay. They start with
a mere topic, move to some easy facts and feelings that
may not pan out, then begin to focus on an opinion that
can be argued. They work on developing support for
that opinion, start to marshal the evidence they will

use, consider how to structure that evidence, and . . . ,
wow—suddenly they have a thesis! Now they can begin
to write something that begins to look and feel like an
essay. Developing a good thesis is hard work, but it
repays the effort. Think how much easier the writing
will be now than it would have been if you had begun
the hopeless and aimless task of writing on something
as unfocused as "Funerals in America"!

CHAPTER 5

FINDING YOUR WRITING PROCESS

No two writers have the same method for getting started in writing, or getting finished. One of your most important tasks as you develop your skills as a writer is to discover your own best writing process. No one can tell you how you do your best writing. Teachers can tell you what they have discovered about their own writing and what their experience with hundreds of student writers suggests about some strategies that seem to work with many beginning writers. But in the end your writing process is your own, and will be in some ways unique to you. As you work out your own most effective process, however, it may be helpful to be aware of some of the processes that work for some other successful writers.

A few writers—very few—get their ideas and their supporting arguments all worked out in their heads, then just write down what turns out to be a first—and perhaps last—draft. For such writers the actual writing—the placing of black marks on a white page—is the last stage in the creative process. It is little more than a boring mechanical act of transcribing what is in the head onto a sheet of paper. Some years ago a colleague of mine refused to learn word processing. "I don't revise," he said. "All I need is a good electric typewriter that will let me lift off and replace an occasional wrong keystroke." For most of us, however, composing essays is far different from that.

Some writers need to work with a pad and pencil. They jot down disconnected phrases, then toss out most of them and select one or two to work with some more. They jot down another mess of ideas, stir them around, beat a few into submission, fluff a few up, and worry that they are doing it all wrong. They finally seize on some approach that seems less stupid than the others, write a paragraph, tear it up, start again. And then again. Soon all they have to show for their efforts are a wastebasket full of garbage and a sloppy first draft.

Still others need to talk it all out first with a friend: "I don't know. I'm not sure I liked that woman we had to interview. Her ideas about when human life starts were interesting, but there was something about her cocksure arrogance that bothered me. I mean, how can I take seriously someone who thinks she has all the answers? How reliable can her ideas be if she gives no impression of ever having had any doubts about a single one of them? Do you think I could write about what a jerk I thought she was?" The friend comments,

"Of course, you don't really know how she reached those conclusions. Maybe they were the result of long and painful searching. Besides, do you want to write about your reaction to her personality, or your reaction to her ideas?" And so on, until finally the writer thinks he has focused the ideas enough to write down a thesis and begin organizing support for it.

Some writers need a picture. The picture might be a central circle labeled *main idea* surrounded by lots of little circles with other labels, and arrows pointing hither and yon. It might be an outline of some sort showing how various seemingly unrelated ideas are related. It might look like a tree with a thick central trunk, a couple of main branches, and lots of little twigs. It might look like a chart or a mathematical formula. For such writers the actual writing becomes a verbalization of the concepts and relationships represented in the picture.

For some writers the computer screen provides the only picture they need. They use the computer screen as a kind of artist's canvas, clicking in words and phrases and sentences as they think of them. They dance from one screen to the next, tapping in an idea here, a fragment there. They pound out a paragraph on "page-up," an example on page 4, a conclusion on "end of document." The screen becomes a kind of disordered mirror record of what is—or was—in their minds. Then they move whole blocks of text—then move them back again. For such writers, putting a draft together may be a matter of deleting the chunks that do not fit the picture that has grown out of their minds, and then writing connectives between the chunks that are left.

All of these approaches, and others, as well, can yield quite excellent essays—or quite mediocre ones. In fact, most of us have not one but a number of different writing processes that we combine or adapt to the kind of writing assignment we have, the length of the piece we are writing, the amount of knowledge we have on our subject, the audience we are writing for, and the amount of time we have for the project. And a good writer knows that the very best writing often has an element of magic to it that is best left unanalyzed. But it is good to stand aside a little as we write, to observe ourselves as we work, so that we can learn a little something about who we are and how we do our most effective writing.

CHAPTER 6

BUILDING A STRONG ESSAY

Like painting and romancing, writing is highly
individual. If everyone did it exactly the same way it
would be neither inspiring nor fun for anyone involved.
Although there is no rigid formula for good writing, it
is possible to learn from our own mistakes and from the
mistakes of those who have gone before us. Consider
the case of Ramon. The setting is Friday, at the end
of English class. English teacher (aloud): "For next
Friday, please submit a six-hundred-word essay on a
current trend gripping America—the fitness trend."
Ramon (silently): "Friday! Wow! That's a whole week
away. But six hundred words? That's about 575 more
than I have to say on the fitness trend. I'll never be
able to write that essay. Never." From that Friday
night to the next Thursday night Ramon lives up to his
prediction, doing nothing. Thursday night he agonizes
for seven hours over what he feels in his heart is the

worst arrangement of words he has ever seen on paper. He counts: 562 words. He adds a few adjectives here, some clauses there: 580. He tacks on a meaningless concluding sentence: "So we can see from this essay that the recent trend in fitness gripping America is a current trend." There: 599. He is tired and figures maybe the teacher will miscount. A week later he gets back his failing essay, feigns surprise, but eventually admits that perhaps he deserved no better. You, however, can learn from Ramon's mistakes.

Writing an essay does not have to be that way. When you are given a full week to write your essay, you should begin right away. The trick is, of course, to start the Friday you get the assignment. Just as you would not expect to turn an out-of-shape body into something resembling a Greek statue in one night, you cannot expect to write a topnotch essay at the last minute. There is a process for building a strong, convincing, well-developed essay. And, like getting in shape, it takes time.

First, do not panic. Panic blocks the thinking channels, and you cannot write if you cannot think. You would not look into the mirror at your weak and out-of-shape body, scream, "Oh, my God! I'm weak and out of shape," and fly into a frenzy. That would not make you stronger. You would think, "I'm going to do something about this." With that resolution in mind, you could begin the process of building a better body. The same goes for building a better essay.

Now that you are calm and your mind is active, you must gather your tools. If you were working on your physique you would need weights, sneakers, a towel. For your essay you need ideas—those tools that you will use to develop a strong essay. Take a clean sheet of paper and a pencil and try brainstorming. Jot down ideas as you would in a word-association game. Your sheet should look messy, with words and phrases running in all different directions—up, down, diagonal, in circles—whatever suits you. You might come up with the following words and phrases: "fitness," "physique,"

THE TRICK, OF COURSE, IS TO START THE DAY YOU GET THE ASSIGNMENT!

"muscle," "Mr. America," "Miss America," "looks," "appearances," "people want to look good," "looks are important," "health," "attract opposite sex."

If this kind of brainstorming does not work for you, you might try another strategy for discovering what ideas you will want to work with. One of these strategies is sometimes called "freewriting." In freewriting you jot down not just words and phrases, but sentences, as you explore your ideas on a certain subject. Keep the freewriting really free. Just spit out sentences as they come to you or as one leads to another. This is not your rough draft. Do not stop to edit as you go. Think of it as a kind of automatic mind dump in which you blurt out ideas and feelings as they come to you. Later you will mine the dump to pick out the brightest gems.

If freewriting does not work, try some other strategy. Try imagining that you are talking with a friend about your ideas. Some of us are more expressive if we have a real audience for our words. Think of your discovery process here as explaining what you feel to a friend, but write down what you are feeling instead of speaking it out loud. Or you might want to try imagining yourself standing up in class giving an impromptu speech to your classmates about a certain subject. Or perhaps you think spatially and want to draw a diagram or something that will look like a road map with towns along the way, or rooms within a house. No one can tell you what your own best method for generating ideas might be. Whatever works is just fine. The point is that you do need to find those ideas and jot them down before you forget them so that you have, in the end, something that might be called an "idea collection" to work with.

Now stand back and look at your idea collection. Perhaps you will see a pattern, a thesis growing from the idea collection: "The current fitness trend in America is sparked not by a growing concern for health but by the increasing pressure to look good in an appearance-oriented world." This sentence may lead you to new ideas. Jot them down: "movies," "movie stars," "videos," "clothing," "designer labels," "fancy cars." These ideas are starting to fit together. You decide to argue in your essay that Americans have become overly concerned with appearance. You decide that the fitness trend is the natural outgrowth of a people whose heroes and heroines are visual images and whose greatest desire is to own clothes with other people's names on them. Your essay is taking shape.

The next step involves more preparation. Just as you would organize a daily workout and diet, you need to organize your developing essay. Think about how you might divide your ideas into paragraphs. Try writing a topic sentence summarizing each paragraph. Perhaps writing each sentence at the top of its own sheet of notebook paper would help you keep your thoughts organized. On each piece of paper, jot down ideas for developing that paragraph. For example, if the second paragraph of your essay is going to detail some of America's obsessions with appearances, you might write some ideas about rock videos, designer clothing, the entertainment spectacles during football halftime shows, and advertisers' use of incredibly thin models. When you are finished, you will have quite a few ideas and still no real writing. But that is okay. You have ideas and an outline, and it is still only Friday night.

Now comes the most difficult part. On Saturday morning start warming up, lifting those weights, beginning that diet, writing that essay. Do not expect too much of yourself at first. Write whatever comes to mind under each of your topics, using the ideas you listed the night before. There is no need to pause for the perfect word, no need to worry about whether "effect" or "affect" is right or whether your subjects and verbs agree. You can return later to settle those issues. For now, just write. The purpose here is to get a draft that will bear some resemblance to the piece you will eventually hand in. When you have finished, when you have written whatever you can for each paragraph, take a break. Put the essay aside for an evening, even two. After all, you would not want to pull a muscle.

Monday or Tuesday might be the right time for a rough-draft conference if your teacher has made arrangements with you for one. Or you might ask a friend to look at your draft and tell you what is puzzling about it, or what part he or she likes best, or what additional support you need, or whether it seems to have a clear and unifying thesis. Or, if you are more of a loner, you might want to set the draft aside for a day or two and then come back to it with fresh—and more critical—eyes. Again, the object is to find someone with enough distance from your work or to find enough time so that you can gain that distance yourself. You need that distanced view to see with your readers' eyes and, so, come to understand better what needs more work.

What does need more work? The arms? The legs? The whole body? Increase your attention to those areas:

develop your ideas; strengthen your points; tune your diction; write another draft if necessary. If you are not happy with the essay, the idea, the purpose or point, throw them all away and start over. If the diet was making you ill, you would find a new one. If the weights were hurting, you might try push-ups. If the essay is making you sick, perhaps you need a fresh approach. Do not be afraid to toss out your first attempts and start anew. If, however, everything feels and looks good, move on to the next step.

Many people tend to ignore or forget editing, but it is important. Take another break and return to your essay the next day—Tuesday or Wednesday. Read the essay once again. Does your basic argument still hold? Would a strong transition help your reader? Change words that do not seem right. Help lost modifiers find their proper homes. If everything looks good and you are satisfied, show the piece to some friends. Say, "How does this look to you?" They will say, "Your writing is great, but you look even better."

Don't forget to proofread. You would not go around showing off your new physique if your hair was not combed. Make that final copy look good. After all, appearances do count in our appearance-oriented society. And you are finished on Wednesday or Thursday, a day or two early. If you have followed these steps—relax, jot down your ideas, write your thesis, organize and outline, draft, draft again, edit, and proofread—you are looking really good.

CHAPTER 7

WRITING TO DISCOVER

Five centuries ago a bold sea captain eager to get rich
set out to discover a shortcut to India. His idea was that
if he sailed west he could avoid that long slow journey
south down the coast of Africa, around the Cape of Good
Hope, and then east to India. His idea was a good one,
given the information he had. The problem was that on
his trip west he bumped into other hunks of land that
kept him from getting to India. Columbus died thinking
he had failed. In a sense he had. It is unfortunate
that he never quite realized that he had discovered
something far more significant than a shortcut to India.
Writing an essay is something like that first voyage
west. Maria starts off thinking she is striking out boldly
toward a noble destination, but she hits impediments.
Things get in her way. They slow her down. They annoy
her. They divert her from her course. Perhaps instead

of getting angry and frustrated, she should pause to see whether those impediments are worth exploring in their own right. It may be that they hold something far more valuable than the spices of India.

Maria drives to college two evenings a week after work. To fulfill a course assignment she decides to write an essay about the problems she encounters on the drive. She is not particularly inspired about the subject, but on the other hand it is something she knows about. She brainstorms for a few minutes and makes a list of the problems that annoy her. First, there is construction on Route 73. The workmen are never working when she uses that road, but their barriers are still up and the one-lane traffic slows her down. Then there is the delayed rush-hour traffic on that two-mile stretch of Lawson Drive between the industrial park and the interstate. And the drivers of those big tractor-trailers who act as if they own the roads. What else? Oh, yeah, the joggers and the kids on bikes. And just tonight there was that farmer, dragging a load of hay on Lancer's Lane, who wound up leading a half-mile train of cars before he mercifully pulled his hay wagon onto a side road. And the parking lot! An acre of empty spaces in the faculty lot right up next to the classroom building, but nothing closer than a half mile away for students.

Maria has three days before she has to turn the paper in, so she knows this will not be her final draft. She has discovered that she has the best success in her writing if she just blurts things out without planning a whole lot, figuring she can change it later if she has to. She starts writing:

Half the Fun Is Getting There. Ha!

There are lots of impediments to getting to class at LCCC. They make me wonder if it is worth it taking these classes. I work hard all day at the plant and then have to hassle with a lot of problems to get to school after work. There are basically two kinds of impediments, physical impediments like road construction and potholes, and human impediments caused by people who are inconsiderate of the needs of others.

It really burns me up to have to crawl along in stop-and-go traffic, passing every ten minutes a sign that says "Speed Limit 45 MPH." We can all understand normal construction delays, but they've been working on that six-mile stretch of road since last Easter. I suppose it is nice that they are adding a lane, but now the road is nothing but an obstacle course of orange cones and white sawhorses and yellow bulldozers. Who needs that kind of nonsense after a day in the plant of having to put up with a lazy and abusive foreman? I don't. It wouldn't be so bad if they just got on with their work, but days go by and I don't notice any progress at all.

And if the construction delays were not enough, I also have to put up with those enormous trucks. I suppose they have a right to a share of the road, but when they obstruct my vision for six miles and hog three-quarters of the road and then make me sit and wait while

```
they seesaw into some little loading
dock someplace, I start to wonder
whether all this is worth it. I mean,
it would be one thing if I knew that
these courses were going to be getting
me someplace, but who needs the hassle
of fighting road-hog truckers just to
take some courses that aren't going to
help me much anyhow? I mean, I will
still probably have that same arrogant
supervisor, only now he will just make
stupid remarks about the "collitch kid"
who works for him.
```

As she writes, Maria begins to see that in her essay she is bumping into obstacles more serious than the orange cones and yellow bulldozers that beset her path to school. What she is bumping into is herself, or, more precisely, her negative attitudes about her job at the plant and her uncertainty about her decision to take college courses. Those obstacles get in the way of her reaching the goal she thought she wanted to strike out for—an essay about how hard it is to get to class. But as she writes she senses that she is being unreasonable. She senses that it is selfish and whiney to complain about efforts to widen the road, about truckers backing up to loading docks, about joggers trying to keep in shape, about farmers hauling a load of hay. But if those are not the problem, what is? If Maria is honest with herself, she will sense that she should be writing about something other than the problems she has getting to class. She will realize that she should be writing not about those external problems she started with, but about the real problem: herself.

Now what can Maria do? Well, she can bulldoze her way through to her original destination, increasingly aware as she does so, that she is sounding self-centered and paranoid about a world that is out to make life difficult for her. Or she can strike out in a slightly different direction and write an essay about her own frustrations with her job and her doubts about her decision to take college classes. What, and waste all that writing she has already done? Not at all. Was it a waste for Columbus to sail to India, just because he never got there? Maria may find that she can build on what she has discovered in such a way that her essay profits from her first little misdirected voyage:

Discovering Myself

As the semester wears on, I find myself increasingly short-tempered about attending college. I leave my job feeling grumpy and by the time I get to class I find myself growing more and more angry. Why do those contractors have to be widening the road I have to take to class? Why does that trucker decide to unload his truck just when it will delay me for two minutes? Why does that idiot jogger have to pick my road to run on? And that stupid redneck farmer—why does he use my road, on my evening for class, to take his load of hay on a wobbly ramble into the sunset? And as for the Neanderthal architect who planned the parking lots at LCCC . . . but wait a minute. Why am I blaming all those innocent people when the real problem is that I just don't want to be driving to

```
class in the first place? I have come to
see that my frustration at driving to
school after work is just an easy way
of avoiding having to admit that I have
grown to hate my job, that I distrust my
supervisor, and that I have lost sight
of the fact that I am attending college
because I want to escape from both of
them.
   I suppose there are some people who
can enjoy a job that demands nothing but
punctuality, a dull brain, and an
ability to stand in front of a moving
conveyor for hours at a time. I suppose
.  .  .  .
```

There are times when writers merely report what they already know. More often, however, writers discover in the process of expressing themselves what they really want to say. For most good writers, writing is far less a question of finding the words than of finding the ideas. Columbus seems never to have noticed that those hunks of land standing in his way were worth exploring. Today we know better.

CHAPTER 8

THE PARTS OF AN ESSAY

A strong essay needs a strong *introduction,* a strong *body,* and a strong *conclusion.* If you have been reading attentively, you will have noticed that each essay I have presented has had these parts, though you might not have thought of them in quite those terms. In this chapter I explain briefly what these parts are and what each part is expected to accomplish.

Your introductory paragraph is obviously vital because it can capture the interest of your readers and make them want to read on. A bad introduction can weaken an otherwise strong essay; a good introduction can strengthen an otherwise weak essay. There are various ways of introducing an essay. Bluntly present your thesis sentence ("Dogs are almost human."). Ask a question ("Why did we lose the tournament last week?"). Say something shocking ("I came close to murdering my father last week."). Say something funny ("It does not bother me that I have eight o'clock classes every morning."). Say something that will involve your readers ("Tuition is going up by another $975 next year."). Say something personal ("I think I am in love with my roommate's father."). Try in your introduction to convince your readers that *you* care about your subject. If *you* do not sound interested in or excited about your topic, you start off on the wrong foot. Whatever you do, do not begin by saying, or even implying, "Well, I don't really have anything to say about this topic, but since I've got to write an essay, I might as well talk about . . . ." It may well be that you are writing only to fulfill an assignment rather than because you have something astounding to tell the world, but you should hide that fact and *pretend* that you have something you want to say and that you are pleased to have the chance to present your argument to concerned readers. I have more to say about introductions in my next chapter, but for now let us glance quickly at the center section, or body, of your essay.

The body of your essay is obviously important because it is here that you set forth your basic argument, present your basic facts, and develop your basic evidence. It is primarily in the body of your essay—the part between the introduction and the conclusion—that your essay succeeds or fails as a piece of argumentative writing. It is here that you develop your thesis, prove your point. The body of an essay almost always requires several paragraphs. These paragraphs, each of which should offer support to your

main argument in the essay, can be arranged in one of
several ways. Because those ways are so important, I
save them for another chapter and move to a discussion
of the concluding section of your essay.

A strong concluding paragraph can help to reinforce
your thesis. There are several ways to conclude an
essay, just as there are several ways to introduce it.
One adequate, but not very imaginative or clever, way
is to give a straight summary of what you have said
in the body of the essay: "We see, then, that Roosevelt
was a great president because he brought America
out of the Great Depression, because he . . . ." A more
imaginative way might be for you to show your topic in
a slightly new light: "Because of Roosevelt's greatness,
America still leads the world in . . . ." You might tell a
little anecdote about how your grandmother cried when
Roosevelt died because she felt that America's greatness
had died with him. Or you might quote an authority:
"In the words of Jack Kennedy, Roosevelt was a great
president because . . . ." Whatever method of concluding
your essay you choose, remember that a conclusion
must somehow reinforce your main point. It must drive
home the point one emphatic last time. There are times,
of course, when the last paragraph of the body of your
essay is sufficiently emphatic that the essay does not
require a separate concluding paragraph.

Most writers know intuitively that they should
avoid trite or rote formulas for beginnings of essays.
That is, there is no standard way to start an essay, like
"To start off . . ." or "As we shall see in the coming pages
. . . ." Why, then, do so many writers settle for a formula

closing by starting their concluding paragraph with
"And in conclusion, . . ." or "We have seen, then,
that . . . ."? Skip the formula and find words that drive
home the argument you have been making. Try to
be creative, but keep in mind that your task is not to
introduce new ideas but to reinforce your main points in
a fresh way. Which of these conclusions do you find most
emphatic?:

> A strong essay, then, as I have said,
> needs a strong introduction, a strong
> body, and a strong conclusion. Each
> element is necessary in order to make
> the essay acceptable.

> Admittedly, the conclusion is the least
> important part of an essay. By the end,
> your reader is tired, maybe even bored,
> and in any case should already have
> grasped your main ideas and doesn't
> really want to hear them all over again.
> Still, you need to think carefully about
> how to end your essay.

> Think of your essay as a red pickup
> truck. Without a strong introduction,
> your pickup won't start. Without a
> strong body, the bed of your pickup is
> empty. Without a strong conclusion, your
> pickup has no destination. If you charge
> the battery, load the cargo, and know
> where that cargo is going, you can drive
> your point home with cheerful confidence.

CHAPTER 9

INTRODUCTIONS ARE
NOT ALL THE SAME

Not long ago I visited a marine museum in Los Angeles. I happened to be there at a time when a member of the staff was giving a brief talk about the grey whales of California. The speaker was a delightful young woman who had spent much of her life since the age of twelve learning about these whales: watching them from the Pacific bluffs; counting them for a whale census; going out in small boats to watch them eat, mate, care for their young, and help each other; pressing for legislation that would protect them from the men of several nations who kill them for profit; studying about them in college courses; doing research on them with one of her college professors. Her lecture was exciting right from the start. How did she start? She did not begin with a joke or a flashy anecdote. She began with an introduction in

which she told her audience what turned out to be the
thesis of her brief lecture—"Whales are a lot like you
and me"—and in which she let us know how she was
going to proceed with her talk:

> Whales, like people, need to be warm and they need
> to eat. Like people—well, some people—they are
> loyal to their friends. Like people, they fall in love.
> And although I have never talked with a whale, I
> am pretty sure that they talk with each other. This
> morning I want to tell you some of what I have
> learned about the grey whales that live out there.
> I want to tell you a little about how these friends
> of mine keep warm and how they help each other.
> And then I want to tell you why I think they fall in
> love and what some recent research reveals about
> the way they talk with each other.

It was a fine introduction. It caught my attention. It
inspired this essay of mine, in which I first describe two
of the primary elements that a good introduction should
have—a statement of your thesis and an indication of
your organizational plan—and then show you how to
turn a weak introduction into a strong one.

Your opening paragraph must announce your
thesis. Because your job is to develop an argument
in your essay, it is essential that you tell your reader
right up front what that argument is. I have frequently
encountered beginning writers who think that suspense
is important and that they should not reveal what their
thesis is until the very end of the essay. There may be
times when this tactic is effective, but almost always
you are better off announcing your basic point right at
the start. Remember that unambiguous clarity is one

of your goals in argumentative writing and that little
is gained by withholding your central point from your
readers. And remember that because part of your job as
a writer of expository prose is to make your reader's job
easy, the earlier you can make your main point clear the
better. If your thesis is that Franklin Delano Roosevelt
was a great president, you are wise to announce that at
the start.

In addition to announcing your thesis, the
introduction should give some indication of how you are
going to develop your essay. In other words, you should
give your readers some clear clues about how the body of
your essay is organized. You can usually give those clues
in a single sentence. It can be a very general sentence:
"Roosevelt was a great president because he influenced
U.S. policy in five important ways." A statement like
that tells your readers that you will discuss those five
ways in five major parts of your essay. It is better
yet if you can be more specific in the introduction:
"Roosevelt was a great president because he brought
the nation out of the Depression, introduced the Social
Security system, and strengthened America's position
abroad." That is a better statement because it tells your
reader exactly how each of your next three paragraphs
supports your main argument.

Let us consider an introductory paragraph written
not long ago by one of my students in response to an
essay topic on stereotyping. Michelle entitled her essay
"Men Are Not All the Same." As you read it, look for a
statement of her thesis and then try—alas, in vain—to
determine how she will organize the body of the essay:

YOUR OPENING PARAGRAPH
MUST ANNOUNCE YOUR THESIS!

Since I chose to write about the ways
women stereotype men, my mind has been
filled with examples too obvious and
too numerous to mention. Actually it
seems that women stereotype men just
about as much as men stereotype women.
I believe that both sexes are forced
into stereotyping the other sex through
the media. Toy manufacturers make dolls
for little girls who will grow up to be
mothers, and toy guns for little boys

```
who will grow up to be men. My mother
fell into the media's trap and tried to
raise what TV and magazines called the
"typical American family." She finally
realized that men are not all the same.
```

This paragraph starts limping from the very first sentence—indeed, from the very first word, for it is not immediately clear whether "since" means "because" or "ever since." Has Michelle's mind been filled with examples *because* she chose to write about this topic, or *ever since* she chose to write about it? More important, if she is not going to mention examples because they are either too obvious or too numerous, why waste the space telling her readers about them at all? She ought to tell us right away what she *is* going to mention in her essay. But we cannot identify her main idea because her paragraph lacks direction, focus, and order. Michelle had not made up her mind which of three possible theses she was going to develop: (1) "women stereotype men just about as much as men stereotype women"; (2) "both sexes are forced into stereotyping the other sex through the media"; (3) "men are not all the same." The three possible theses are related, of course, but to develop any one of the three would be quite sufficient for an essay; to try to develop all three in the same essay would be chaos.

To revise this introduction, Michelle had to decide which of her three alternative theses was really going to be the focus of the essay. She took the second alternative: the media are responsible for women's stereotyping of men. Once she decided on that approach, she had to decide how she was going to develop that topic. Once she had done that, she was ready to write the introductory paragraph. Notice that her revised paragraph now focuses on television, not the more abstract "media":

> Television has had the effect of making women stereotype men just as much as men stereotype women. This fact is obvious enough when we think of all those American women watching all those Hollywood films that are continually aired on television. In these films men rescue children, climb mountains, fight wars, go on safaris, seize criminals, and always, always get the girl. It is less obvious that the sportscasters, newscasters, and advertisers on television also tend to portray a macho image of men. A consideration of the way men are portrayed by these three groups of television personages will demonstrate that women who watch television can scarcely be blamed if they stereotype men.

Michelle now shows a firm control over her material. There is nothing extra, no wandering around, no leaving it to the reader to guess which of two or three different topics she will discuss. Michelle knows exactly what her thesis is. She is ready to get on now to her paragraph on sportscasters. And so are her readers.

It is usually best to write a strong introduction before you start the body of your essay, so that the thesis will be well set in your mind and so that both you and

your readers know how you will proceed to develop
that thesis. Sometimes, of course, you will change
your mind as you write, and shift either your thesis or
your organizational plan. If you do make such a shift,
you will want to go back afterward and rewrite the
introduction. Regardless of how many times you rewrite
it, however, your introduction is an instrument of
amazing power. It can help your readers to identify your
main point and give them a preview of your supporting
points. Or it can cloud your main point and leave your
readers lost in a fog of disordered thoughts. Make sure
you write your introduction in such a way that its power
works in your favor. Your readers will thank you.

CHAPTER 10

SOMETHING OF SUBSTANCE TO SAY

Back when I was describing the six qualities of an acceptable essay, I squeezed in a phrase that you probably did not notice—about how to write an acceptable essay: "To write one of those you must, of course, have something of substance to say, and you must use proper grammar and decently constructed sentences. Beyond all of that, however, an acceptable essay is a bold, clear, and well-developed argument presented in a unified, cohesive, and organized form." At that time I did not emphasize the expression, "something of substance to say" because I did not want to distract you from the other points I was making. But now I want to talk some more about what I mean by substance in an essay. Substance is not easy to define, yet most of us know it when we see it. It gives an essay a certain heft or significance, a certain involvement or

commitment, a certain thoughtfulness or intelligence.
But those are merely words. Let me try to give those
words meaning by discussing examples of three student
paragraphs about pollution.

The first is by Roberto on the danagers of pollution:

```
    Pollution is dangerous to people.
This can take the form of air pollution
and of water pollution. The air
pollution is caused by many things,
such as cigarettes, cars, and aerosol
cans. Water pollution is also caused
by many things, such as badly treated
sewage, oil leaks, and illegal disposal
of hazardous wastes. Both air pollution
and water pollution can do serious harm
to human beings, and if not checked it
will do even more harm in the future.
Something must be done. If local, state,
and national legislators do not do
something about pollution, and do not do
it in the very near future, pollution
will cause serious dangers for future
generations to deal with.
```

Roberto's paragraph is well-enough written and is
accurate enough. But surely it is obvious to any reader
that it lacks substance. It is made up of safe truisms
that no one would ever think of denying. It rehashes
the same "dirty old pollution" stuff we hear every day.
It contains no personal involvement, no deep concern,
no commitment. Roberto seems to know little, to have
thought little, and to care little about pollution of any
kind. He does not seem convinced that pollution is a
danger for him or for people of his generation but rather

talks vaguely about it as something "future generations" will have to deal with. He feels that he should present some kind of "solution" to the problem of pollution but can do no more than make a general call for politicians to "do something" about the problem. There is nothing to make any reader think about pollution or do anything about it. We have learned nothing and are inspired to do nothing because the paragraph has no substance.

Let us look at Maya's paragraph on word pollution:

```
We all know about air pollution
and water pollution and even noise
pollution, but no one talks about
another kind of pollution that is
potentially more serious than any of
those. I am referring to word pollution.
I sometimes feel that I am bombarded
by words. The Sunday newspaper I got
yesterday weighed four pounds. I did a
rough estimate by counting the number
of words on an average page of the
newspaper and multiplying that by the
number of pages. I discovered that the
Sunday paper was bombarding me with
approximately one million four-hundred-
thousand words, or three-hundred-fifty
thousand words per pound. I felt that
I was drowning in a sea of words. Then
I turned on the radio to the "all-the-
news-all-the-time" station and got
bombarded once again: "Give us twenty-
two minutes and we'll give you the
world," the announcer says. What he
gives me is a truckload of more words.
So I turned on the television and there
were all those evangelists heaping
```

```
more words on me about scriptures and
goodness and light. Word pollution is
choking America. All we really want on
a Sunday morning is a little peace and
quiet, but with all those words flying at
us, how can we survive until Monday?
```

Maya's paragraph has some substance to it. She has done some thinking about pollution and has come up with an original approach to it, an original species of it. She has even done some research on the number of words in a Sunday paper. Her examples are specific. She has a definite radio station in mind, and she mentions a particular kind of Sunday morning television program. She cares about her subject and enjoys writing about it. She makes me think. Unfortunately, what I wind up thinking is that that "word pollution" is not such a good phrase for what she is talking about. Unlike the air we breathe and the water we drink and the noise we hear, we can all easily avoid the words Maya speaks of. If she does not want those millions of words in the Sunday paper, she does not have to buy a copy. If she wants that peace and quiet she says she wants on a Sunday morning, why does she turn on the radio and the television in the first place? And she never does show that word pollution is "potentially more serious" than the other kinds of pollution. Complaining about "word pollution" is a little like going to a peanut store and complaining about peanut pollution or going to the seashore and complaining about wave pollution. In the end, then, Maya is playing games with her topic. She has not really thought it through, and she stays, finally, on the surface.

Tom takes an international perspective on pollution:

    Americans who have lived in China
do not complain about pollution in
America. Americans who have lived in
China know what it is like not to be
able to drink the water—virtually any
water—without boiling it. And this is
not just because we are foreigners not
used to the local bacteria. The Chinese
do not drink the water without boiling
it because they know it could make them
sick. They know about the untreated
sewage and the industrial pollutants
that flow unchecked into many rivers
and aquifers in China. Americans who
have lived in China know what it is
like to be afraid to inhale because
doing so makes them cough. Americans
who have lived in China know what it
is like to be afraid to go outside on
overcast days because their eyes burn
in the unfiltered smoke from a score
of nearby factories. Americans who
have lived in China usually come home
enthralled with the magnificent scenery
they have viewed, awed by the antiquity
of a society with a five-thousand-year
recorded history, and enamored of the
warm and friendly Chinese people they
have become acquainted with. But they
come home with a new perspective on
the "problem" of pollution in America.
Having seen what real pollution is,
they appreciate being able to drink
tap water and to breathe air that has
almost no lung-poisoning muck in it.
To Americans who have lived in China,
complaining about pollution in America

```
is a little like complaining about the
chocolate in a Snickers bar.
```

That third paragraph has substance. Tom brings a truly new perspective to a tired old topic. He is committed to his subject and conveys both knowledge and a sense of concern about it. He has made me think about some things I had not thought much about before, and he has made me realize something I had not realized before. I come away from that paragraph having learned something about both China and America. Unlike Roberto, Tom makes me want to read more that he has written. I do not care much for his reference to the Snickers bar, but I can forgive that awkward analogy in a paragraph substantial enough to prove that its writer is intelligent, perceptive, and original.

CHAPTER 11

SPEAKING OF VOICE

The writer of every essay has a voice. When we speak of the "voice" of a writer we mean not the spoken voice, but the tone, attitude, posture, or personality that the writer conveys. A writer's voice can be friendly or cold, sincere or sarcastic. None of these voices is necessarily wrong, but some are better than others when we consider the writer, the situation, the message, and the audience. We have a large measure of control over our spoken voices. Our voices can be shrill, or angry, or sweet, or dripping with cynicism. Similarly, we have a large measure of control over our written voices. To show what I mean, I present below four examples of the different voices a writer might use when writing introductory paragraphs about alcoholics. Try to imagine each example as the lead-in to an argument about alcoholics.

Sally's voice in the following paragraph is factual and scientific. There is little of her own personality in it.

She deals with facts and figures, and she tells us where
she got them:

> Anyone can abuse alcohol, but the
> term "alcoholic" is reserved for the 10%
> of the population who are genetically
> predisposed to become addicted to
> alcohol, even when imbibing it in
> small amounts. That 10%, however, is
> not an across-the-board 10%. In some
> groups—Jews and Italians, for example—
> fewer than 1% will become addicted to
> alcohol, no matter how much they drink.
> In other groups—most Native American
> groups, for example—as many as 80% or
> 90% of those who drink become addicts
> or "alcoholics." At least that is what
> James R. Milam and Katherine Ketcham
> report in their book, *Under the Influence*
> (New York: Bantam, 1981). . . .

Scientific Sally's voice is quite appropriate in many
settings. For an audience that just wants the facts, or
that wants to know little about the writer personally,
that voice is just right.

In the next paragraph Alan's voice is much more
distinctive, much more personal. Quite the opposite of
the dispassionate scientist, he is deeply involved in his
topic and tells us his personal experience with it:

> To me an alcoholic is just a polite
> word for a drunk, and I hate drunks. No
> doubt there are some quite lovable and
> harmless drunks. No doubt somebody's
> perfectly nice best friend is a drunk.
> But speaking from the narrow perspective
> of my own experience, I have no reason

not to hate drunks. I have only known
three drunks up close, and that is
plenty for me. One of them ran through a
red light and killed a pregnant woman.
The second lost a fine job at the bank
and then walked out on the family she
could no longer help to support. The
third routinely beat his son—my best
friend. The subject of drunks is not
a subject I want to be reasonable and
humane about. I just want them out of
here. . . .

Angry Alan's voice has the virtue of being honest, and
it does get our attention. Still, to write in such a voice
may be counterproductive because Alan risks alienating
his audience. Such anger can be effective only for an
audience that hates alcoholics with an anger matching
his own. Most readers, feeling that alcoholics deserve
a measure of pity for being caught in the grip of an
obsessive addiction, will react in ways opposite to the
way Alan intends.

In the following paragraph Harry's voice is light,
flippant, funny:

People have strange ways of following
instructions. I told my alky buddy Bert
not to scratch my car, so what does he
do? He ties one on, skids sideways into
a fire hydrant, and dents in the door.
"See," he says. "No scratches. You
didn't say nothing about dents." That
reminds me of the one about the alky
in Peeker's Bar who ordered a martini.
He drank the martini, then fished out
the olive and put it in a jar. Then he
ordered another martini, drank it, and

> put the olive in the jar. Then he did
> it again. Pretty soon the bartender got
> curious and asked him what he thought he
> was doing drinking all those martinis
> and saving the olives. "Well, ish
> like thish," the alky says. "I'm juss
> follerin' structions. Wife tole me to go
> git her a jar of olives, and thash what
> I'm doin'!". . .

We all like a good joke, but Humorist Harry had better
be careful. He seems more interested in getting a laugh
than in making a point. With his derogative term
"alky" and his pitiless portrayal of alcoholics as devious
and irresponsible, he undermines his credibility as a
person who can say anything much worth reading about
alcoholics. His voice could conceivably be appropriate
if Harry were an alcoholic himself and was addressing
an audience of fellow alcoholics. In that situation his
humor would be directed in part at himself. I can
imagine, however, no other audience worth addressing
that would be profitably addressed in this voice.

Carla's paragraph is written in a sincere, serious,
self-reflective voice:

> My mother is an alcoholic. Right
> now she is what is called a recovering
> alcoholic. She has not had a drink
> in three years. We have something
> like a family life again, and I can
> say—honestly this time—that I love
> her. But there was a time not so long
> ago when she was not recovering. There
> was a time when I was getting sucked
> down that alcoholic sewer with her. I
> started acting crazy. I lied, telling

the neighbors Mom had the flu again. I
went on search-and-destroy missions all
around the house to find the bottles of
stuff that was poisoning her. And when
Mom had her stupid little car accident
that sunny Sunday two blocks from home,

DIFFERENT WRITERS, DIFFERENT VOICES.

```
I wished that she rather than the car
had been totaled. The car was some good
to someone. Mom? She was no good to
anyone. And neither was I. . . .
```

Confessional Carla's voice may not be for everyone, but most readers will appreciate her brutal honesty. It is tough to admit that she hated her own mother and wished her dead. It hurts to dig up the kinds of memories Carla uncovers for us. Carla comes across as a concerned, caring person who wants to tell her story, possibly to help others who may be in a situation similar to hers. Perhaps what is most winning in her voice is that, unlike Angry Alan who had directed his hostility at alcoholics, Carla is willing to admit that she was as crazy and useless as her mother had been.

Notice some of the elements that contribute to the variety of voices here. Something as simple as word choice is key. Is the subject of our discussion someone "genetically predisposed to become addicted to alcohol," "a drunk," "an alky," or a "recovering alcoholic"? Changing the words changes the voice. And consider the stance of the speaker. Does she stand far away in a library, like Scientific Sally, speaking of segments of the population, or does she, like Confessional Carla, stand right there next to her mother? Does he, like Angry Alan, distance himself through hatred or, like Humorous Harry, through jokes? Changing the stance changes the voice. My point is not that any of these four voices is wrong, any more than a shrill or gruff or deep or quiet spoken voice is wrong. Any of them might be right in a certain set of circumstances. Sometimes we want to be scientific and make no reference to our own personal beliefs and experiences. Sometimes we want to be silly or even cynical. Sometimes we want to be confessional. One of the many choices writers have to make is which voice is most appropriate to the situation we are writing about and the audience we are writing for. We want to engage our readers, not unnecessarily annoy or alienate them. I would not say that Carla's voice is "better" than that of Sally or Alan or Harry, but I do find it more appealing. I would like to hear more of what she has to say, and I think I would enjoy meeting her. Those other three voices make me wonder whether I should stop listening to their arguments about alcoholics.

CHAPTER 12

ORGANIZING YOUR ESSAY

The body of the essay is crucial. Without it there would be nothing to introduce and nothing to conclude. The two major concerns you must have when you think about the body of your essay are, first, what you are going to say and, second, how you are going to organize what you say. I cannot help you much with the first, for only you can know what you have to say. I can, however, help you with the second by suggesting some ways to organize essays. The only general guidelines for organizing an essay are that (1) you must have an organizational principle in mind for the body of the essay, (2) you must identify a principle of organization that will most effectively convey your ideas to your readers and convince them that your argument is valid, and (3) you must make that principle apparent to your readers in your introduction. There are many methods

of organizing an essay. In this chapter, I discuss five of
the most versatile and useful methods, five methods you
will find yourself turning to time and again to say what
you want to say in your writing. These methods are
listing, cause and effect, definition, classification, and
analysis. I illustrate each method very briefly by telling
you how a writer might use each one to organize an
essay about love, a topic so broad and so universal that
it readily admits of diversity of approach.

The first and simplest method of organization is
enumeration, or *listing.* I am employing this method
now by listing five of the most useful ways to organize
an essay. Indeed, several of the chapters in this book
are organized as lists. In my chapter on "Nervous
Grumblings about Writing," for example, I list a
series of complaints I have heard beginning writers
make about writing. Rarely are lists mere random
collections of points or ideas, however, for there is
usually an internal logic to the order of the list: from
least important to most important, or from oldest to
youngest, or from general to specific. In an essay about
love you might decide to list the various attitudes
toward love that the other students in your class seem
to have: contempt, amusement, unconcern, passionate
involvement, and so on. Listing is usually the simplest—
and least imaginative—form of organization, and you
should use it sparingly. It is the right method only if
what you want to say lends itself readily to this format.
The danger often is that your list will not serve to
develop an arguable point you want to make, or that
the items will not really work well together to build a

unified essay. You may wind up with just a list rather
than with a fully developed argument.

A second method is organization through *cause and
effect.* My chapter on "Your Thesis Sentence" might be
seen as a cause-and-effect essay, for there I tried to
show the effects of various alternative thesis sentences
on the work involved in writing an essay. Use this
organizational method when you want to discuss either
the causes or the effects of a given phenomenon. You
might begin with a cause and discuss the effects of it
or you might begin with an effect and then discuss its
causes. You might for example, discuss the effects of
the American concept of love on the capitalist system:
is the great American profit motive enhanced by
American ideals of brotherly love? Or you might talk
about the causes of the decline of love in America in
the last two decades or the causes of the increased
divorce rate between 1950 and 2010. When you use the
cause-and-effect method of organization, be cautious
about oversimplification. Are you sure one thing caused
another? Are you sure you have included all of the
important effects?

A third method is organization through *definition.*
The typical pattern here is to offer a capsule definition
of a term or concept and then in the body of the essay
expand on various aspects of that definition. You have,
of course, seen me do just that in my chapter defining
an acceptable essay: *a bold, clear, and well-developed
argument presented in a unified, cohesive, and organized
form.* The body of that essay, then, expands on the six

important terms in that definition. If you could think
of a workable definition of love, you might try the same
approach, but defining something as abstract as love
is difficult. More manageable would be a definition of
the term *lover*. In any case, use this method sparingly
and with great caution, for it can lead to bland formula
writing. If you define a lover as "a person who feels
affection, concern, and desire for another person," my
response is, "So what else is new?" Be sure to avoid
circular definition: "A lover is a person who loves
someone." If you do use this method, try to be original:
"A lover is a young man who has finally found someone
he likes better than his rusty 1959 Ford."

A fourth way to organize an essay is by the principle
of *classification*. Classification usually involves division
of a subject into several classes, or groups. I used this
method, along with definition, in my chapter detailing
the components of an acceptable essay. Recall that I
classified the essential qualifications of a good essay into
two major subgroups: those three having to do primarily
with the subject of the essay and those three having to
do primarily with the form of the essay. If you wanted
to classify the various kinds of love, you might come up
with six classes:

> Romantic love (love of a person not one's relative);
> Spiritual love (love of one's God);
> Patriotic love (love of one's country);
> Sibling love (love of one's brothers and sisters);
> Filial love (love of one's parents);
> Love of nature.

You would probably find six to be a rather unwieldy number for an essay, and that it would be better to reclassify these six into two subgroups of three each:

> Love of humans (romantic, filial, sibling);
> Love of nonhumans (God, country, nature).

Having done that, you would probably find that you could deal with only one of the two subcategories in an essay. Keep in mind, of course, that classification should not be an end in itself in your essays. It is not likely that your instructor will assign an essay topic in which you are asked simply to divide or classify something. Instead, he or she will give you a topic in which classification may be one of the methods of organization that you might use, *if* it helps you argue your point. In talking about the effects of love on women, for example, you might find it convenient to classify women into three groups: never married, married, and previously married. In that case, by the way, you would be doing what writers often have to do: combining two or more methods of organization. Classification of women would be used to advance an essay on the effects of love.

A fifth way to organize an essay is through *analysis.* Two kinds of analysis usually concern us in essay writing. The first is analysis into parts—sometimes called structural analysis. I used this kind in my chapter on "The Parts of an Essay": introduction, body, and conclusion. The second kind of analysis is process analysis or analysis into steps. I used this kind of analysis in my chapter on "Building a Strong Essay": relax, gather ideas, develop a thesis, and so on. You may have noticed that in my chapter "Introductions Are Not All the Same" I used both kinds of analysis. First I used structural analysis to show the two elements to be found in an acceptable introduction. Then I used process analysis to show how Michelle transformed a weak introduction into a strong one. Let us consider an example or two of possible uses of analysis in essays about love. If you were to consider what elements really constitute romantic love between men and women, you might find it useful to break down romantic love into three parts: physical attraction, intellectual attraction, and emotional attraction. That would be structural analysis. Or you might want to outline the step-by-step process by which people fall in love: first, recognizing beauty or handsomeness; second, discovering similar interests; third, . . . , and so on. That step-by-step analysis would be process analysis. You will find that you use analysis a great deal in your own essays—in such topics as how to avoid getting sick on campus food, how to juggle going to college and working full time, the parts of an M-l rifle, the composition of a glacier, the character of Captain Ahab, and how to drive your English teacher crazy.

There are other ways to organize an essay than these five. For example, we have the *chronological* method and the *comparison-contrast* method. These two methods are of sufficient importance that I devote the next two chapters to a more extended discussion of them. But there are other methods as well that I do not discuss. You will discover those as you read other writers' essays and as you develop strategies for arranging your own arguments. The point is that because you cannot blurt out everything you want to say all at once, you must find a method for dividing your material into units you can deal with conveniently in a paragraph or in a major section of a longer essay. In making that division you must select the method that allows you to present your argument most clearly and efficiently.

CHAPTER 13

THE CHRONOLOGICAL APPROACH

One of the giveaway signs of inexperienced writers is their tendency to write chronologically rather than conceptually. They describe a series of events one after the other, leaving to their readers most of the work of analyzing those events. It is natural to think and write chronologically. Doing so can be an important part of the process of discovering what argument we want to make, but writers must not fall into the comfortable chronological habit. To do so can be a serious miscarriage in communication, because readers may come away from a chronologically arranged narrative with quite a different set of concepts than those the writer had in mind. I present three chronological accounts from student papers, and I show how the

writers might have used some of the same materials to
support a series of clearly defined concepts.

Here is Paul writing about his life:

> My earliest memory of my father is
> the time he spanked me for unrolling
> a whole roll of toilet paper into the
> toilet. He not only spanked me, but
> he made me reach in with my bare hand
> and take out all that paper. I hated
> him for that. I guess I was around five
> years old then. Another thing I remember
> about him was the time he marched me in
> to my teacher—I think I was in second
> grade—and asked that the teacher give
> me some chores to do after school to pay
> for the arithmetic book I had ruined by
> leaving it outside on a rainy night.
> Another early memory I have is the time
> he made me watch when he butchered one
> of our sheep. I do not remember how old
> I was then—maybe around ten or eleven.
> Anyhow, that was a pretty unpleasant
> experience, because on our farm we had
> raised that sheep from a lamb.

Here is Jamilla writing about science:

> We went to four locations near the
> campus and collected three samples of
> soil from each. The first was in the
> woods up near Moorestown, north of
> campus. The second was in a farmer's
> field that had been used for corn for
> at least the past two years, over by
> Topton. The third was in the abandoned
> gravel pit down by the river just east
> of the campus. We collected three

samples from each location, one at
the surface, one six inches below the
surface, and one twelve inches below the
surface. The first thing my group did
was take the various soil samples that
we had collected in the field and, after
carefully labeling them, dried them out
in a hot oven (350F) for thirty minutes.
Then we measured out exactly equal
portions of each of the nine samples, by
volume (.75 cc). Then we weighed each
sample. After that we took a pinch of
the dirt and examined it under a sixty-
power microscope.

And here is Tony writing about a short story:

In John Cheever's "The Swimmer"
an athletic man named Neddy decides
to "swim" home. He stands on a hill
and looks down across the valley and
decides that he can go from that spot
to his home by swimming through the
swimming pools of a lot of his friends
and neighbors. At first this seems very
strange, because why would anyone want
to do that in the first place, but then
it seems more logical. Neddy is a social
type of person as well as an athletic
one and he wants to have a chance to
talk to all of his neighbors, rather
than just walk or run home alone on the
streets. The first pool he comes to is a
very festive one. The owners are having
a garden party, and Neddy stops to have
a drink and talk with a couple of his
friends before he dives into the pool,
swims to the other end, and climbs the

```
fence to the next yard. At one of the
pools he talks with a woman he had once
had an affair with, but then he swims
through her pool and goes on to the
next. When he gets home he discovers
that his house is abandoned.
```

Those three samples are all written chronologically. Writing chronologically is relatively easy because it requires little analysis on the part of the writer, who writes merely what happened first, then what happened next, then what happened after that. Almost all of the transitions relate to time: "first," "next," "the following Friday," "and then." The chronological approach to writing comes naturally to us. For most of us, our first experience with reading was chronological: "Once upon a time . . . ."; "Times grew worse and worse with Rip Van Winkle as years of matrimony rolled on. . . ."; "Young Goodman Brown came forth, at sunset, into the street of Salem village. . . ." Almost every television show is written chronologically. What could be more natural, after all, than starting at the start and ending at the end? But though the chronological approach is often the best one for telling a story or giving directions, it is usually the worst for argumentative or expository writing. Unless your purpose is to explain how something is done, a step-by-step process, you are better off steadfastly resisting the temptation to organize your essay chronologically.

Writing chronologically may be a necessary first step for some writers who are searching for an idea, a thesis. As a method of organization for the final paper, however, the chronological method is one of the weakest. One problem is that it is too seductive: it tempts writers to wander on and on, mentioning fact after fact, event after event, experience after experience. It is too easy for writers to avoid the rigorous thinking that they need to do for effective argumentation. To put the matter another way, the chronological approach focuses the attention of readers on the order of events, not on the importance of the events. To put it still another way, chronological writing too often leaves to readers, not to the writer, the hard work of figuring out what the events in an essay mean, figuring out what the thesis is, figuring out the concepts. To write chronologically is too often to write confusingly.

Let us nudge Paul and Jamilla and Tony into trying again. This time we want them to subordinate to a governing concept some of the interesting and useful events they mentioned in their chronological account. Here is Paul, writing once again about his life experiences, but this time using them in service to an argument he wants to make about his father:

> I suppose my father was mean to me, but I have come to see that his meanness was really an expression of love. But how was I, a five-year-old boy, to see any love in a scowling face telling me to reach into the toilet and fish out with my bare hands the icy wad of toilet paper I had unrolled into it? How was I to know in the second grade that there was love in that stern man's insistence that I work after school to pay for an

arithmetic book I had left out in the
rain? How was I to know, a couple of
years later, that it was love that made
him insist that I watch him butcher a
sheep, because he wanted me to know that
the meat I ate did not grow, wrapped in
cellophane, on trees. Surely, however,
it was love. I know now that it *was* love
that prompted my father to insist that
I be responsible for cleaning up my own
messes, pay for my own irresponsibility,
and learn about food and death. Another
man might, in his love for his son, have
cleaned up my mess, paid for my book,
and shielded me from unpleasant truths,
but is it really love to prevent a child
from learning and growing?

Here we see Jamilla writing about those scientific
discoveries, but putting them now into a context that
makes it clear why she needs to report her findings:

The most interesting discovery
that we made was that the topsoil is
lighter in weight and finer in texture
in locations where the ground has not
been disturbed. We made that discovery
by analyzing nine soil samples that we
collected near the campus. We dried
the samples, then carefully weighed
them and analyzed their texture under a
microscope. The practical implications
of our experiment are of interest to
farmers, conservationists, and . . . .

And here we see Tony describing Neddy's strange
swim. Now, however, instead of just telling us random
chronological events in the story, he selects the events

that help him to prove a point about Neddy's mental
state:

> If we define a crazy person as someone
> who is out of touch with reality, then
> surely Neddy in John Cheever's "The
> Swimmer" is crazy. His craziness shows
> up in his imagining that a series of
> ritzy swimming pools is a river, which
> he even names the Lucinda River. That
> craziness shows up even more obviously
> in his refusal to accept the fact that
> his wife and children have left him and
> that the bank has foreclosed on his
> house. How could anyone who was sane
> believe . . . .

Notice what our writers have done in each case here:
provided a context in which the discussion of certain
events serves a clear purpose. Paul is not just telling
us about vague memories of his father; he is telling
us about how his father showed love in unusual ways.
Jamilla is not just describing, out of context, a series
of steps she went through in a science experiment; she
is telling her readers what was important about what
she learned. Tony is not just telling what Neddy did;
he is using what Neddy did to reinforce a conclusion
he has drawn about Neddy's mental state. Our lives
are a series of chronological experiences, but we need
not be slaves in our writing to the order in which those
events took place. As we grow more experienced in our
writing, we learn to analyze those experiences, to draw
conclusions from them, and to write in such a way that
they become support for clearly articulated concepts.

CHAPTER 14

COMPARING AND CONTRASTING

One of the most useful ways to organize an essay is comparison-contrast. This method can be used to point out similarities between two apparently unlike objects, persons, or concepts, or to suggest differences between two apparently similar objects, persons, or concepts. It can also be used in an argumentative essay to show the various ways that one character or idea is better than another. If you use comparison-contrast, it is important to realize that there are two ways to organize such an essay: the *divided* pattern and the *alternating* pattern. The first of these is less likely to serve your purposes as a college writer than the second. Whether you use the divided or the alternating pattern, however, you must remember that comparison-contrast is a means to a persuasive end, not an end in itself.

The *divided* pattern is the one I used in my last chapter, "The Chronological Approach." In that chapter I was contrasting the chronological approach with the conceptual approach because I wanted to show why the second was better. An outline of that chapter would look like this:

I. The chronological approach
   A. Writing about one's life
   B. Writing about science
   C. Writing about a short story
II. The conceptual approach
   A. Writing about one's life
   B. Writing about science
   C. Writing about a short story.

This pattern is called the divided pattern, obviously enough, because the two approaches being contrasted are separated, or divided. The first half of the body of the chapter is devoted to the chronological approach, and the second half is devoted to the conceptual approach. Although this pattern can sometimes be effective, particularly in a very short essay, certain difficulties are inherent in it. One problem is that it can readily make the essay seem to fall apart into two separate, disconnected essays. Another is that readers can too easily forget when they get to the second set of examples what the content of the first set was.

The second pattern, called the *alternating* pattern, is more likely to be useful in college writing. It is called the alternating pattern because the writer in each part of the essay alternates from one item compared to the other. If I had chosen to write that last chapter according to the alternating pattern, the outline would have looked like this:

I. Writing about one's life
    A. Chronological approach
    B. Conceptual approach
II. Writing about science
    A. Chronological approach
    B. Conceptual approach
III. Writing about a short story
    A. Chronological approach
    B. Conceptual approach.

The advantage to the alternating approach is that you would have read Paul's conceptual account of his father's treatment of him as a child immediately after you had read the chronological account. The contrasts I pointed out would have been clearer if you had read the two examples next to one another.

Let us consider another example. Kurt is going to write about why young people should consider a career in teaching rather than a career in business. Setting aside the question of financial rewards, he decides to concentrate in his essay on the intangible rewards of a teaching career. After mulling the matter over, he concludes that teaching is likely to be more rewarding because it will give him more independence, more opportunity to influence people, and more time to spend with his children. He could set the essay up in two ways. One is the divided pattern:

  I. Business
    A. Independence
    B. Opportunity to influence people
    C. Chance to spend time with children
 II. Teaching
    A. Independence
    B. Opportunity to influence people
    C. Chance to spend time with children.

But Kurt could more effectively prove his point if he set
his essay up in the alternating pattern:

   I. Independence
    A. Business
    B. Teaching
  II. Opportunity to influence people
    A. Business
    B. Teaching
 III. Chance to spend time with children
    A. Business
    B. Teaching.

With this second method Kurt could help his readers
focus on his thesis by organizing his essay to emphasize,
in each of the three large parts of his essay, the three
intangible advantages of teaching.

Whether you use the divided pattern or the
alternating pattern, beware of a potential trap—that
of doing an idle comparison-contrast essay just for the
sake of the exercise. Comparison-contrast, like the
other methods of organization, is a means to an end,
not an end in itself. Use it if it helps you to develop your

argument. Do not simply list four ways that two things are similar or different and think you are finished. Those four ways must help you to reinforce a central

COMPARISON-CONTRAST IS A MEANS TO AN END...

point or argument you are trying to make, such as that
the conceptual approach is more effective than the
chronological approach, or that the alternating method
is more effective than the divided method, or that a
career in teaching has many benefits that a career in
business does not have, or that falling in love is very
much like climbing Mount Everest.

CHAPTER 15

DEALING WITH
THE OPPOSITION

Implicit in much that I have been saying in this book is that most of the writing you do in college and in the professional world is, finally, argument. For the most part you are writing to convince your readers that you know something worth sharing, or that your views on a certain subject are reasonable, or that your readers should take some course of action. Most college students seem to have pretty good instincts about formulating their arguments. You know that to prove your points you have to give evidence and be logical and reasonable in your presentation of that evidence. What you may not realize, however, is that to be an effective writer, you should present only the evidence in favor of your own point of view and suppress any mention of arguments on the other side. To mention the evidence on the other side is unwise for three reasons: (1) it tells readers that your conclusions may, after all, be wrong; (2) it makes you seem uncertain and wishy-washy; and (3) it wastes space that you could better spend on arguments in favor of your point. Right? Not necessarily. Although there is a certain commonsense logic to this reasoning against presenting both sides in the argument, I have found over the years that I am generally much more likely to be persuaded by writers who spend some of their time refuting—or at least acknowledging—the major arguments of their opponents. Let us consider each of those three reasons in more detail.

Although it may sometimes be risky to mention the arguments against your own view because your readers might find those arguments more convincing than your own, it is even more risky to appear ignorant or arrogant by pretending that there are no such arguments. One of my beginning writing students wrote a paper in which he argued that first-year students should be permitted to have cars on campus. Hakim wrote about how much more convenient it would be if first-year students had cars so that they could do their laundry off campus in less crowded laundromats and so that they could rush home if they got word suddenly that a family member was sick. At the end of the essay, however, Hakim had still not mentioned any of the key arguments *against* letting first-year students have cars on campus: most first-year students adjust more quickly to college life if they are encouraged to stay on campus during weekends rather than go home to their parents and high school buddies; cars are expensive to operate and maintain; there is not enough parking on campus as it is, let alone with a thousand more cars vying for parking places. In the end, Hakim came across sounding incredibly naive because his silence about the arguments against cars for first-year students led me to suspect that he simply had not thought of those arguments. How could he expect to convince me if he seemed unaware of even the most obvious arguments against his point of view? Writers who appear uninformed cannot hope to persuade.

Just as you need not pretend that there are no valid arguments against your view, so you usually need not worry about sounding unconvincing or wishy-washy in mentioning those arguments. If you keep a proper balance between your pros and your cons, your reader is likely to be impressed that, though you are fully aware of the arguments against your view, you are more persuaded by the stronger arguments for it. Another student of mine wrote an essay arguing that every college campus should have a family planning center. Sharon admitted that having such a center might upset members of certain religious faiths, and that other students and their parents might fear that its mere presence could lead to a destructive promiscuity among students. Despite all that, Sharon said, a family planning center would benefit many students. The center, she argued, would help to provide information about the physical diseases and the unwanted pregnancies that are such a routinely troubling aspect of the lives of sexually active college students. In the end, I found Sharon's arguments to be all the more convincing because she had admitted at the beginning that she was aware that there were some valid arguments against a family planning center on campus. Writers who appear to be closed-minded cannot expect to persuade an open-minded audience.

If you need not be overly concerned about losing your case by mentioning arguments on the other side, nor about appearing uncertain or wishy-washy by doing so, how can you avoid the risk of spending so much space acknowledging the opposing points that you have too little space to argue for your own views? The answer is simple: you can avoid that risk by spending more space arguing for your own view than acknowledging the arguments in favor of the other side. There are several ways to keep a proper balance. One way is to do what I have done in my introduction and to state—or overstate—the opposition view as if it were your own, then deny it. Another way is to do as I have also done in this chapter: mention the major arguments against your own view and then systematically refute those arguments, one by one, in the body of the essay. Still another way is to use your introduction to acknowledge the opposite view, then not mention it again and proceed with your own arguments. For example, Kurt might begin an essay on the advantages of a career in teaching over a career in business in this fashion:

```
    I always thought that I wanted to be
a businessman, just like my father, but
I am growing increasingly less certain.
I am becoming more and more interested
in becoming a teacher. There is no
denying, of course, that I could almost
```

```
certainly make more money in business
than in education. I am coming to see,
however, that balancing the advantage
of more money are a series of less
tangible benefits that come to teachers.
Among the most important of these
benefits are . . . .
```

Kurt need make no further reference to the monetary advantages of a life in business. By acknowledging that advantage in a sentence at the start, however, he has shown that he is not totally starry-eyed or naive about his subject. By admitting the major argument against his view right at the start, he has earned the right to devote the bulk of his essay to those intangible benefits of teaching.

In a sense, failing to take into account the opposing arguments is a failure to respect the intelligence of your audience. Hakim seemed to think that no one reading his essay was smart enough to figure out that there might be good reasons for not allowing first-year students to have cars on campus. Sharon, on the other hand, respected her readers enough to realize that they could present a case for the thoughtful and caring people who might object to having a family planning center on campus. Writing an argument is a little like taking part in a debate. All good debaters know that they must spend most of their debating time arguing positively and aggressively for their own side of a proposition. They also know, however, that they must show an awareness of and a respect for the other side. Because almost all expository writing involves arguing for a certain point of view and because no proposition is worth arguing if it is not possible to argue the other side as well, you can learn from debaters that it is often wise to admit that the opposition has some valid arguments. Doing so either sets up an opportunity for you to refute those arguments or else lets you suggest that, valid as those arguments are, your own arguments for the other side are even more convincing.

CHAPTER 16

LOOK AT YOUR AUDIENCE

More than once in the course of this book I have talked about your readers—how to make your points clear to them, how to persuade them, and so on. The question of audience is a vexing one, particularly for college writers who have to write for an English teacher. I would like to talk generally about the question of audience and then help you to imagine an appropriate audience for your essays.

It does, of course, matter who your audience is because you will write differently for different audiences. Consider an example. Assume that you are writing a description of the tree outside your window. You would say one thing if you were describing it in a letter to your mother to give her an idea of how pretty your new apartment is. You would say something else if you were describing the tree to a biologist friend in order to find out its genus and species. You would say

something else entirely if you were describing it to your
lover because you wanted him to know that everywhere
you looked you saw his face, even in that tree outside
your bedroom window. You would say something else
if you were describing it to a painter who wanted to get
just the right shades of green on a canvas, something
else if you were describing it to a blind man who had
never seen a tree, something else if you were describing
it for a newspaper audience in an editorial about how
terrible it is that such trees are cut down to make paper.
And so on. In each case the tree you describe would be
exactly the same one, but the way you write about it
would differ drastically depending on your audience.
The same is as true for argumentative writing as for
descriptive writing. If you were asked to write an essay
about the problem of stray dogs on campus, you would
take one approach with a society for preventing humans
from being cruel to animals, another with the student
government subcommittee on academic environment,
still another with the local police. You can supply from
your own imagination examples to demonstrate the
different kinds of essays that would result from your
writing for different audiences.

Who is your audience for a college essay? In a sense,
of course, your reader is that remarkable creature
known as your English teacher. He or she will usually
be the final audience for your essay, and have to
comment on it and assign it a grade. But your teacher
is really an artificial sort of reader. If you are writing
about your apartment, or about students having cars
on campus, or about corruption in politics, your English

teacher has no power to do much about any of these
situations. He or she is a kind of "pretend" audience,
someone who will serve as your temporary or trial
audience until you begin doing the kind of writing for
which you will have a "real" audience.

My advice, however, is that you think of your
classmates, not your English teacher, as the audience
for your essays. They are your peers, and, depending on
how your teacher structures the class, they may well
have an opportunity to read and comment on some of
your essays. As you write, then, imagine that you are
writing for readers of your generation who go to the
same college you go to, who are just as concerned about
getting decent grades as you are, who are reading the
same English books you are reading.

But do not get complacent in your writing. If you
imagine your audience as people in just the same cozy
club you belong to, with the same tastes in music, the
same life goals, the same political views, the same
opinions on feminism, your writing will lack purpose
and conviction. Most often when we write we want to
inform or to change the opinions of our audience. As you
imagine your readers with the same general background
as you, then, imagine also that they are different
from you in their knowledge and opinions about the
subject you are writing about. If you are arguing that
the president should have expanded powers to declare
war, imagine readers who think that only Congress
should declare war. Your job as a writer is to convince
them that they may have been hasty or unreasonable
in their views. If you are writing about a novel you

really enjoyed, imagine readers who have read it, just as you did, but who hated it, or who were bored by it, or who misunderstood its central theme. Your job as a writer is to make them hate it less, or be less bored by it, or understand its point. As for Kurt's essay on the

advantages of a career in teaching, if he imagines as
his audience a group of students who have decided that
they want to be teachers, he will not challenge himself
to persuade students thinking of a career in business
to reconsider their values. Imagine an audience of your
peers, yes, but peers whose views you must influence
in some important way. Imagine an audience of peers
who strongly disagree with you initially, but who, like
you, are willing to read all the way to the end of a clear
argument that challenges their original view. Imagine
an audience of peers who, like you, are capable of being
persuaded by careful logic, reasonable examples, and
strong evidence.

And what do these peers of yours want to see in your
essays? That is easy: they want to see just what you
want to see in their essays. Like you, they are bored by
the perfunctory "I've-got-to-write-this-stupid-essay-so-
here-goes" approach. They like it when someone tells
them something they did not know or gives it a slant
they had not thought of. They enjoy being amused.
They would much rather read a bold, clear, and well-
developed argument presented in a unified, cohesive,
and organized form than read one that is wishy-washy,
muddled, skimpy, disunified, choppy, and disorganized.
They resent having to read an essay twice just to figure
out what the main idea is, only to discover that there
is none. They are insulted by sloppy, careless writing.
They like essays that stand on their own six paragraphs
better than ones in which the writer assumes that they
have memorized an encyclopedia of the horse or know
what the coefficient of the obverse tangent is. They care

less where the commas are than what the ideas are, and they want those ideas expressed in lucid, simple, and honest prose. They think of writing as a means by which writers convey meaning without drawing attention to themselves or to any lovely words or sentences they are using to convey that meaning.

Writers have struggled with the question of audience for years. Warren Buffett, head of the conglomerate holding company Berkshire Hathaway, Inc., and one of the wealthiest men in the world, wrote the preface to *A Plain English Handbook* (first published in 1998 by the U.S. government's Securities and Exchange Commission). In that preface Buffett said: "Write with a specific person in mind. When writing Berkshire Hathaway's annual report, I pretend that I'm talking to my sisters. I have no trouble picturing them. Though highly intelligent, they are not experts in accounting or finance. They will understand plain English, but jargon may puzzle them. My goal is simply to give them the information I would wish them to supply me if our positions were reversed." That's excellent advice for you, too. Imagine as your audience someone who is as intelligent as you are, but who is not an expert on the subject you are writing about. Apply the Golden Rule of writing and write as plainly and as directly for others as you would have them write for you. In other words, as you imagine your audience, glance into the mirror. You may not think that person is all that lovely, but your audience likes pretty much what that imperfect person in the mirror likes in an essay.

CHAPTER 17

WRITING WITH OTHERS

Much of the writing done in the professional world is collaborative. A research team puts out a report on its findings about a new concept in biofeedback. A government subcommittee makes recommendations about a better way to monitor voting machines. A medical unit is asked to explain the hospital's policy on heroic measures for the terminally ill. A junior partner and a law clerk work together on a law brief involving a client's alleged tax evasion. An engineering team writes the construction specifications for a new shopping mall. A bank vice president writes a draft of a major policy speech for the executive vice president who reads it, likes the first half, but wants the second half revised to reflect the tougher insurance laws. In the professional world few important documents are solo efforts. Out there, writers collaborate—literally co-labor—with others. But what about student writing? Is it, also, collaborative? Much of it is; more of it probably should be. Every time you ask a parent or a friend to read a draft of your paper and suggest ways you might improve it, you are engaging in collaborative writing. There was a time when receiving this kind of help might have been considered a mild form of plagiarism, but that is no longer so. Many writing teachers encourage students to get help with their writing. Indeed, they often institutionalize that help in various ways.

One way to institutionalize collaborative writing is for your teacher to call you in for an individual conference, sometimes called a rough-draft conference. Typically you bring a first or second draft of your essay with you. Your teacher may, in your presence, read over your draft and ask you certain questions about what she sees. She may offer some friendly words of encouragement and perhaps suggest that in your next draft you might offer additional support for some of your points. Or she may ask if you are pleased with the voice you project in your essay. She may suggest that you review the rules about comma splices before you turn in your final draft. Because this conference takes place before she evaluates your revised work, she has become your collaborator—your co-writer.

If your school is lucky enough to have a writing center or writing lab, you may want to visit it. Depending on the way it is set up and the kinds of services it offers, you can probably either call for an appointment or just drop in to talk with one of the tutors. The staff of the writing center can help you bring focus to your ideas, can help you understand certain of

the finer points of grammar, can help you control your
tendency to wander away from your thesis. Your work
with the tutors at the writing center is a collaborative
effort.

Your teacher may spend class time in collaborative
class exercises. She may feel most comfortable with
large-group discussions. Perhaps she will read aloud,
show on an overhead scanner, or distribute copies
of an essay that you or one of your classmates has
written. Having done so, she may ask members of
the class to share their reactions to it. In doing so she
may encourage them to comment on the strengths and
weaknesses of the paper, or to suggest ways the writer
might make its thesis more compelling. Such comments
and suggestions are collaborative in nature.

Or perhaps your teacher may feel more comfortable
working with smaller groups or in-class workshops. The
idea in such groups is to encourage students to act as
an early audience for each other's work. What happens
in these small groups is sometimes called peer criticism
or peer review. These peer sessions can work in various
ways, but typically students work during peer sessions
in groups of four or five. They read each other's drafts
and give either oral or written critiques of their fellow
students' work. This collaboration is usually done before
the teacher sees your essay. The idea is for you to get
some early reactions to your draft from your fellow
students before you make final revisions on it and turn
it in. Some teachers ask to see the earlier draft of your
paper, the comments made by your peers, and the draft
of your essay responding to those comments. Some ask

that you append a brief acknowledgments section telling who helped you with your paper.

To see how peer criticism works, let us assume that Kurt's peers take a look at his essay on the advantages of a career in teaching over a career in business:

> A career in teaching offers greater independence than one in business. Teachers have something called "academic freedom," which means that they can say or do anything they want in their own classrooms. Unlike businessmen, teachers don't have a boss hanging over them all the time telling them what to do, when to do it, and how to do it. Furthermore, teachers are freed from the need to show a financial profit every month. They are free to experiment, to take risks that may not pan out. They are free to answer a higher calling than the call to drag in more and more cash.

Kurt's peers might offer the following comments on this paragraph: "I like what you are getting at, but you seem to shift from 'independence' to 'freedom.' Are they really the same thing?" "Do you really want to be so hard on business careers, Kurt? I mean, businessmen take risks, too, and many of them have a higher calling than just more cash. If they did not, they'd fail for sure." "Isn't the word 'businessman' sexist? Lots of women are in business now." "I don't know, Kurt, but aren't you romanticizing teaching pretty much? Don't teachers have some sort of bosses—like principals, deans, or something? And don't they have some kind of monetary responsibility to taxpayers, or tuition-paying parents, or anyone?" "I guess I'd like to see an example or two in there, Kurt. I mean, it seems all kind of general." "Could you compare not teachers in general and business people in general, but, say, the independence of a teacher of banking with the independence of a bank manager?" In the end Kurt might not take all of that advice, but his essay will be much better if he takes some of it.

Students occasionally object to peer criticism. They feel uncomfortable and inadequate criticizing the work of other students, and they do not quite trust the opinions of other students about their own writing. "It is the blind leading the blind," they say. Most teachers understand such feelings, but they know that one of the best ways to gain knowledge and confidence as a writer is to read the writing of others with a critical eye. I have found over the years that students are quite good indeed at giving sensitive and sensible readings of the work of other students. What they lack in experience and confidence they make up for in freshness of instinct and honesty of response. We all know the miracle of the blind carpenter who picked up his hammer and saw. Peer criticism is built on another kind of miracle: the miracle of blind students who lead each other to see better what effective writing is.

Miracle or not, collaborative writing is here to stay—especially among the most serious writers. A glance at the preface of nearly every book shows that most published writers want to acknowledge the help

they have received: "I am grateful to _____
who first suggested the idea for this book. Without
_____'s careful reading of an early draft of
the manuscript, this book would not have taken on
the present shape. As always, my primary debt is to
my spouse _____, whose loving but tough
criticism has touched virtually every page." The names
change, of course, but authors want to say thanks to
those who have helped them. They know that their
work would probably not have been good enough to
be published if they had worked entirely alone or had
arrogantly denied the validity of the suggestions made
by others.

CHAPTER 18

STANDING ABOVE
OUR DEFENSES

Defense mechanisms are wonderful. They enable us
to live with our own inadequacies by blaming other
people or conditions over which we have no control. We
all, of course, have inadequacies, and most of us can
function most effectively if we find ways not to dwell on
them. If you get a more negative response to your essay
than you expect, it is natural and probably healthy to
rely on one defense mechanism or another. One of the
most popular is to blame the evaluator: "What does he
know, anyhow?"; "She just doesn't like my style."; "He
completely missed the point of my essay!" Another is
to blame the topics: "How can anyone write decently
on *any* of those stupid subjects?"; "Where in the world
does she dig *those* topics up?" A third is to blame the
circumstances: "I just can't function well in the early

morning."; "Deadlines! They absolutely paralyze me. How can I possibly be creative when there is a deadline hanging over me?"; "I wasn't able to concentrate because I had a big physics test the next day." And so on. If it is any consolation, we teachers have our own defense mechanisms that help us to cope with our failures as teachers: "Students these days are impossibly dense."; "Damn television anyhow! How can students learn to write if they never read?"; "Don't those high school teachers teach *any*thing these days?" And so on. There is no point in trying to eliminate defense mechanisms because, of course, they *do* defend us, and often enough there is some truth in them. It is sometimes useful, however, to try to stand a little above our defenses. To help you do that, let me suggest several ways you might react productively to what may seem to you to be a discouraging evaluation of your writing.

For one thing, you might want to remember that your readers—your peers and your teacher—are collaborators trying to help you. Even when that help takes the form of what seems to you a negative comment, their intent is still to help you learn to write better. Kurt has the final say about what shape his paper will take, but he is wise to take all suggestions and comments seriously. His readers can help him better than anyone else can by pointing out the weaknesses he needs to work on and the ways he can attack those weaknesses in an effort to improve his writing.

No comment, positive or negative, can help you if you do not reread your own essays. You will usually

IT IS SOMETIMES USEFUL TO STAND ABOVE OUR DEFENSES...

get your essay back within a week after you turned it
in. Forget that *you* wrote the essay and read it the way
you would read a classmate's essay. As you read, try to
think of the essay as *writing* but not *your* writing. Then,
when you read the comments, keep in mind that the
evaluators are commenting on your *writing* and not on
you. A negative comment has nothing to do with *you*.
It is not your readers' business to evaluate you. It is
their business to evaluate—however subjectively—your
writing.

   The evaluation, of course, *is* somewhat subjective,
and therefore it may be inaccurate, prejudiced, or
unfair. But however subjective that evaluation may
be, it is almost sure to be more objective than your
evaluation of your own writing. Think of your readers'
comments as a means of helping you understand what
impression your essay has made. You may know what
you *meant* to say, but your readers are in a far better
position than you are to determine what you actually
did say. If your readers missed your point, it may be
that they are not too bright. It may also be, however,
that you did not make your meaning clear, or that your
argument drifted from its original direction, or that
your organizational pattern was confusing, or that you
left out an important piece of evidence, or that you did
not think your essay through as carefully as you might
have. If you insist upon thinking of your readers as
unintelligent and your own writing as brilliant, you are
being highly subjective, and you will not improve much.
Even brilliant writers have room for improvement, and

surely no brilliant writers got that way by ignoring advice from their readers.

The best defense against negative evaluations, of course, is to write good essays. Your peers and your instructor, for all their imperfections, weaknesses, and failures, can, more than anyone else you know right now, help you learn to do just that. Can you let your defense mechanisms down just a little so you can hear those friendly voices giving you all that constructive criticism? If you can, you will discover that as your writing improves those voices say ever kinder things about it as the term goes along. It would be a shame to miss those compliments.

CHAPTER 19

A HEALTHY
BODY PARAGRAPH

Although there is almost infinite variety in the
paragraphs good writers compose, most of the
paragraphs you need to write for the body of your essays
have three elements: a topic sentence, sentences that
develop the topic sentence, and a transitional device.
Experienced journalists, authors, and business writers
frequently write quite acceptable paragraphs without
one or another of these elements, but you will do well
to make sure that all three are in the body paragraphs
you write for college courses—unless you have good and
specific reasons for excluding them. Without all three,
most body paragraphs seem weak or crippled. Let us
consider each of these elements in more detail.

A topic sentence is to a paragraph what a thesis
sentence is to an essay. It is a single sentence that

states the central topic or point of the paragraph. A
topic sentence need not be either very long or very
short. It must, however, state what the paragraph is
about, its one main idea. A paragraph in the body of
an argumentative essay is by definition a collection of
related sentences that support a single point. The topic
sentence states what that single point is. That single
point, of course, should be itself a piece of support for
the thesis or larger point of the essay as a whole. The
topic sentence of a paragraph, that is, must be related to
and extend the thesis of the essay. This topic sentence is
often built into the opening sentence in the paragraph.
Occasionally it is the final sentence in the paragraph,
in which case it serves to conclude, tie together, or
summarize a series of related earlier sentences.
There are times when it appears in the middle of the
paragraph, with a sentence or more leading up to it
and a sentence or more explaining or commenting on it.
There may even be times when the topic sentence is so
obvious that the writer leaves it unstated. You have to
be an experienced writer, however, to know when you
can get away with that, and even then you run the risk
that some readers will miss what seems so obvious to
you.

In addition to the topic sentence, you need other
sentences to develop, or to prove, or to explain the
topic sentence. There are various ways to focus these
sentences, depending on the kind of paragraph you
are constructing: you can give examples; you can tell
an anecdote that illustrates your point; you can cite
evidence from a book you have been reading; you can

quote an authority on your subject; you can apply logical reasoning to support your basic premise. The way you develop a particular paragraph will be determined by the needs of the paragraph, but the central point here is that you must *develop* your topic sentence, that you must provide sentences supporting the central point the topic sentence states. I have more to say about supporting sentences in the next chapter; meanwhile, let us move on to a discussion of the third important element in a paragraph.

In addition to a topic sentence and sentences supporting that topic sentence, you need some sort of transitional device to provide cohesion between the paragraph and other parts of the essay. This device signals to your reader that you are shifting to a new part of your subject and shows how the new paragraph relates to the rest of the essay. Sometimes a single word like "and" or "but" or "however" or "therefore" or "first" or "second" or "third" will do. A short phrase is usually better: "on the other hand," or "still another example," or "the most important evidence, however," or "despite all this negative criticism." A more effective transitional device can be a whole sentence: "Now let us consider the cons of the Democratic party's welfare program." The best transitional sentence is often one that repeats or restates the thesis of the essay: "If we consider the reactions of today's students to the basic engineering curriculum, we find that students also think it is inadequate." You may have noticed that I used a one-sentence transition in the paragraph you are now reading, for I began by repeating the previous two points before mentioning the third: "In addition to a topic sentence and sentences supporting that topic sentence, you need some sort of transitional device." You may also have noticed that in the final sentence of the preceding paragraph I included a transition not only to this paragraph but also to the next chapter. There are many ways to provide transitions, but remember that you almost always need some word, phrase, or sentence to link one paragraph with the ones around it, to give cohesion to the larger building blocks of your essay.

Perhaps an example of a good paragraph would help clarify what I am getting at. Here is Kurt's second body paragraph on the advantages of teaching over business:

> In addition to allowing more independence than a career in business, a career in teaching offers the chance to influence people. Most teachers deal with students at a time when they are most receptive to new knowledge and to changes in values. Most men and women in business, on the other hand, deal with older adults who have already lived through their most impressionable years. In the course of a thirty-year career, teachers have a chance to influence not merely younger people, but also a great many more people than most men and women in business do. If teachers see an average of one hundred different students each year, that makes some three thousand individuals they can influence in a lifetime. How many men and women in business careers have so many opportunities to help their fellow human beings? The real story is told not in

```
the ages or the numbers, however, but
in the individual cases. My high school
mathematics teacher changed my life. Mr.
Simmons helped me during my parents'
divorce, at a time when I was in danger
not only of failing math but also of
dropping out of school altogether. By
caring enough to pay some attention to
me, Mr. Simmons saved me in ways that
no bank manager or sales representative
ever will. I want to be a teacher in
part because I want to "pay back" my
debt to Mr. Simmons by helping others.
If I help save even one student as Mr.
Simmons helped save me, I will feel that
I have repaid that debt.
```

That is not a brilliant paragraph, and it could profit from some friendly peer criticism, but it is an essentially healthy paragraph, and it has the three elements I have been speaking of.

Without a topic sentence your paragraphs lack unity; without supporting sentences your paragraphs lack convincing development; without transitional devices your essay lacks cohesion. A paragraph without unity, development, or cohesion cannot convey your argument effectively.

CHAPTER 20

DOCTORING A
SICKLY BODY PARAGRAPH

In this and the next chapter I show you how to doctor sickly paragraphs and nurse them back to health. This doctoring, you will see, usually involves both surgery (removing unnecessary or diseased parts) and rebuilding (adding tissue to give the patient muscle and strength). Many years ago I made an early-semester assignment in my first-year writing class. This was quite a while back, not long after Lehigh University made the historic switch from being an all-male to a coeducational institution. In those days residence halls were called "dorms," essays were called "compositions," and first-year students were called "freshmen." The assignment to my students was to write a paper about their first impressions of Lehigh University. I told them that they had considerable freedom to limit or adjust the topic so that they could say something interesting about their first impressions of college life, and I told them that I loved details. Here is the paragraph a student named Manfred wrote near the beginning of his essay:

> Leaving home and going to college is both a sad and exciting experience. My father went to Lehigh and he has always wanted me to come here, though most of my friends went to CUNY and I felt sad about not going with them. Moving to Bethlehem from New York City was a shock to my system, for I had not realized how small it was and how few theaters, museums, and other cultural centers it had. College is different from high school. There are so few women at Lehigh that I felt as if I was moving into a freshman monastery of some sort.

The primary problem with this paragraph is that it lacks unity. Notice that the first sentence—the topic sentence—is hopelessly overloaded. It has far too many elements in it: leaving home *and* going to college are sad *and* exciting. With so much to be proved, it is no wonder that Manfred drifts even further in his second sentence by telling us that his father went to Lehigh. He gets back on one of his tracks by stating that it is *sad* to be separated from his friends who are going to another college, but then he quickly drifts off again into the *shock* of coming to Bethlehem. Note that suddenly he is talking about the city, not the university, and that the *shock* he speaks of is different from both the *sadness* and the *excitement* that he had announced in his opening sentence. Then he slips again in the final

sentence by talking about the relative scarcity of women
at Lehigh, which is not obviously relevant to sadness,
excitement, *or* shock. In short, the paragraph runs
off in too many directions. Manfred knew that he was
trying to say something about what it felt like to come to

DOCTORING SICK PARAGRAPHS INVOLVES SURGERY AND REBUILDING.

Lehigh for the first time, but he never quite figured out what he wanted to say in the paragraph, what argument he wanted to make to his readers. He did not realize that he had the seeds here for two or three whole essays in that little paragraph, and that by cramming too much into it he was choking it to death. Before he could begin to unchoke it, to let it breathe more freely and be able to say something, Manfred needed to consider how the paragraph might fit into an essay.

Manfred and I had a brief conference. After considering that the assigned topic was "First Impressions of Lehigh University," Manfred saw that he had really shifted the topic slightly—and quite appropriately—by having decided to focus on his own reactions rather than on Lehigh. He saw that three emotions were dominant in his first days at college: sadness, excitement, and shock. In isolating those three emotions, he saw that he had the basis for a whole essay, not merely a single paragraph. After thinking about the topic some more, he wrote a thesis sentence for the essay, focusing on a more limited and manageable topic, and decided to deal with only his first impressions of residence hall life at Lehigh:

My First Impressions of Dorm Life

Thesis sentence: On my first day in the dorm my feelings changed from sadness to shock, and then to excitement.

Note that Manfred wisely isolated some of the items from that glutted original paragraph so that he could now treat each separately.

Here is what Manfred wrote in his paragraph on shock, the second paragraph in the body of his essay:

```
    I remember the shock I felt when I
first saw my room. It was nothing like
the one I had seen on my campus tour
months earlier. I was also shocked when
I discovered that my roommate seemed to
have an objectionable personality. I
also got a shock when I tried to take a
shower and discovered that the hot-water
control was broken.
```

That paragraph is better. The sadness and the excitement are taken out. There is no reference to leaving home, no reference to Manfred's father's attendance at Lehigh, no reference to the number of women at Lehigh, and none to the lack of museums in Bethlehem. All three sentences mention the *shock* of something directly connected with residence hall living. The unity, now, is there. But the paragraph is not yet a healthy one. Though it now has a clear opening topic sentence ("I remember the shock I felt . . . .") it lacks the other two elements we spoke of earlier as necessary ingredients for body paragraphs: support and a transitional device. We readers do not know what was shocking about the room. We do not know how the room differed from the one he had seen on the campus tour. We do not know what was objectionable about his roommate's personality. We do not know what was shocking about a broken shower handle. Manfred needs to develop all of these ideas with concrete, specific support if he wants his readers to understand what was shocking about his first day in his residence hall. As for

transitions, there are none, and we get no notion here
that this paragraph is part of any larger whole. Manfred
tried again:

> The sadness I had felt when my
> parents walked way from my room gave
> way to shock as I looked around my new
> "home." I saw that it was a far cry
> from that spacious, brightly painted,
> tastefully furnished room I had been
> shown on the campus tour in November.
> The walls had probably once been white,
> but now they were a smeary gray. There
> were many places where last year's
> occupant had pulled patches of paint off
> when he took down his posters. There
> were no curtains on the window and no
> bulb in the wobbly lamp that tottered on
> the scratched-up desk I would be using
> for a year. As I was brushing off a
> cobweb in my dank closet my new roommate
> came in. "I see you are a cleanliness
> freak," said his pimply face. "I hope
> ya don't mind if I smoke sometimes. I
> smoke Marlboros. Say, I got a great jazz
> collection. Jazz soothes me when I go
> to bed." I hate smoking, jazz grates on
> my nerves, and I despise big—mouthed
> braggarts. I grabbed my towel and went
> down to take a shower. The shock as the
> cold water hit me when the hot-water
> control handle came off in my hand was a
> fitting end to a terrible start.

Manfred now almost had it. Perhaps some of the
examples more fittingly demonstrate *disappointment*
than *shock*—is it really *shocking* to find that one's
roommate smokes?—but let us not quibble.

The paragraph now has a clear transitional device taking the essay from the sadness that was the topic of the previous paragraph to the shock that is the unifying topic of this one. The paragraph has specific, concrete supporting sentences. Now, finally, it says something reasonably memorable about Lehigh and about Manfred's initial impressions of residence hall life. Manfred has cured his sickly paragraph. He has given it a focused topic, has supported that topic, and has provided a transitional device. His paragraph is now healthy and strong. And as for us readers, we are delighted because all of a sudden we *see* what was shocking about Manfred's first day in college.

CHAPTER 21

GOOD WRITING IS GOOD THINKING

The primary impediment to good writing is sloppy thinking. You can memorize all the rules of grammar, win every spelling bee you ever entered, and be willing to spend countless hours on every essay, but if you do not take the trouble to think clearly and carefully about what you are saying in the essay, you will fail to write well. The paragraphs we analyzed in the last chapter demonstrated the problem of sloppy thinking clearly enough, but I would like to drive the point home once more by having you diagnose with me the problem in a paragraph taken from an essay by a student named Ann.

The Student as Convict

Summertime is usually a fun time, but after being sentenced to four years at

a correctional institution (sometimes
called college), summertime only means
work: three months of hard labor. All
convicts must work all summer to raise
enough money for some of the expenses at
college, which include a cell, tuition,
and penitentiary-style meals. After
the hard-labor period, it's back to
the process of being transformed from
a "freaked-out punk" into a "straight-
and-narrow" executive. If a convict
is already the "straight-and-narrow"
executive type, he usually has it fairly
easy. The correctional advisers make
sure that the person will have been
completely transformed by the end of his
sentence. Advisers make sure of this by
tracing his progress through the honors
list and the warden's list.

The basic problem here is obvious: sloppy thinking. The
first half of the paragraph deals with what students
do in the summer, whereas the second half makes no
reference whatever to summer work. More important,
Ann is trying to draw an ill-conceived comparison
between the student's life and the convict's life. Is it
really fair, for example, to suggest that a student's
summer job is similar to the hard labor which some
convicts are required to do? As Ann indicates, the
student works for money; the convict does not. There are
problems of logic with the second half of the paragraph
also, for the analogy between students and convicts
again falters. A residence hall room is really not a cell
for no one is locked into it, and there are no bars on the

windows. Ann offers no parallel in the convict's life to
the tuition that she says the student must pay. And,
most puzzling, she speaks of a college's function as one
of rehabilitating "freaked-out punks" (whatever they
are) into "straight-and-narrow" executives. And if that is
not puzzling enough, she makes it even more mystifying
by suggesting that some student-convicts are already
straight-and-narrow executive types when they come
to college—in which case they would presumably need
no "rehabilitation" and so would not need to be at the
"correctional institution" in the first place. I make no
comment about the "warden's list" in the final sentence,
except to say that I am not sure what Ann means by the
term.

In a conference with Ann I asked her how fully she
had thought through her analogy between students
and convicts. "Not very well," she replied. "I just didn't
have much to say on any of your topics. I guess I just
was feeling sort of trapped by this place, so I thought
I'd see where that trapped feeling took me. Not too far,
I guess. Sorry." "No need to apologize," I said. "I find
your basic analogy quite intriguing, but you need to
think it through some more. There is just too much that
doesn't work here. For your next draft, why not think
some more about *the feelings* of a student-convict. Those
feelings may be more convincing than the facts you try
to bring out in this draft." Here is Ann's rewrite:

> To understand why some students drop
> out of college, we must understand that
> they feel somewhat like convicts. They

```
feel that they are in college not by
their own choice but because someone
else—their parents or a guidance
counselor—insisted that they come.
They feel that they are incarcerated
in a rigidly policed institution to
which they have been unjustly sentenced
for four years by a set of social
values they do not accept. They feel
that college is making them over into
something professionally respectable,
just as prisons try to rehabilitate
convicts into socially acceptable
citizens. Occasionally one of these
students stops and says, "Hey, wait!
College is not a prison, and it is silly
for me to stay here and feel like a
convict. I am going to exercise a right
that convicts do not have and drop out
of this place."
```

There is a vast difference between Ann's original version
and her second one. This second try now has unity
because the paragraph sets out to answer—and does
answer—the question of why some students drop out
of college. And it now has a certain logical consistency
in suggesting an analogy between the student and
the convict. No longer does it make the illogical and
unprovable assertion that students *are* like convicts;
instead, it makes the more defensible suggestion
that some students sometimes *feel* like convicts. The
revised version, then, is a pretty good paragraph
because it begins with a defensible topic sentence, it
then offers support for that topic sentence in a series
of more detailed analogies, and it suggests a reason for

the comparison between students and convicts: this comparison will help readers to understand why some students drop out of college.

The revised paragraph has another important feature that the original one did not have: order. It has order because there is a plan to it. It begins with a statement that some students drop out because they feel like convicts. It develops that statement by mentioning three parallels such students see between their own situation and that of the convict. And it concludes with a statement from a typical drop-out student in which she indicates that, since she is not really a convict, she has the freedom to leave. Notice that the triple repetition of the words "they feel" connects the three major parts of the analogy by means of a structural parallelism that helps hold the paragraph together. In summary, the revised paragraph is a much better paragraph because Ann did some clear thinking.

CHAPTER 22

GOOD WRITING IS
GOOD DEVELOPMENT

Any system can be misused. I occasionally encounter students who think they have mastered the "Writing Matters" approach to college writing and proudly turn in essays that have structure but show little development. A first-year student named Steve, for example, wrote the following essay in response to a topic assignment about required attendance at college classes:

To Go or Not to Go

Mandatory attendance of classes at the college level, especially at a college of high distinction, should not exist because students are mature enough, intelligent enough, and responsible enough to decide when and if to attend class.

At this and other prestigious institutions of higher learning students

are selected for admission because they
are from the upper part of their high
school class and very active in sports
and other activities, such as band or
chorus. They are mature enough to handle
their own schedule, so they should not
be required to attend class if they
don't feel they need to.

Also, they are selected to attend
good colleges like this because of their
above-average intelligence. Being that
intelligent, they should be allowed to
decide for themselves whether or not
they have to attend a class, even if
they know the material upside down and
backward.

In addition, most students here are
very responsible or they would not have
been able to obtain the credentials
for admission, such as good grades and
high Scholastic Aptitude Test scores.
If they were responsible enough in high
school to know what they needed to do
or find out, they should still be that
responsible when they arrive at college.
Therefore, they would know what classes
need work and religious attendance, and
which classes don't.

Since students here are selected
because of high intelligence, maturity,
and responsibility, they should be left
alone to decide if they should attend
class, and if they don't attend they
should face the possible consequences of
bad grades. This would give students a
more realistic view of the outside world
because no one forces you to go to work.
You just get fired.

I turned that essay back to Steve with the following comment:

> You seem to have grasped the basic elements of structure in an essay, Steve, and the writing here is grammatically clean. But I wish you had paid more attention to your categories and your development.
>
> First, you seem not to have thought through your categories very carefully. Is there really a distinction between "maturity" and "responsibility," the subjects of the first and third parts of the body of your essay? And why do you mention the SAT scores in the section on responsibility? Wouldn't they more accurately be said to measure intelligence than responsibility?
>
> Second, you have not developed any of your points adequately, for you give almost no examples. As a result, your paragraphs are general, abstract, and bland.
>
> If you don't know what I am talking about, please drop in for a conference. It's important.

Steve did come in. He had reread his essay and understood, he said, about my first point. He admitted that he had had difficulty stringing out his one little point into three.

"Why did you think you had to do that?" I asked.

"Well, because I had to figure some way to have separate paragraphs supporting my main point. They didn't seem to be very separate by the time I got done, though. I had a problem with the logic of my essay, too."

"What's that?"

"I kind of argue in circles. I say that students are mature enough to make the right choices about class attendance, but the only evidence I give is that they wouldn't have gotten into college if they weren't mature enough to make the right choices. Another problem is that at the end I undercut even that reasoning by admitting that some students may *not* make the right choices and so will have to pay the consequences."

"You got it, Steve. You don't need me on that part, do you?"

"No, but I don't understand what you mean about developing my points. I can see that those paragraphs are skimpy, but what else is there to say without just repeating myself?"

"Who wrote that essay?"

"I did. What do you mean? It's not good enough to have been plagiarized, is it?"

"I didn't mean that. I mean there is nothing in it that any of your classmates might not have written, nothing that makes it Steve's paper rather than Tom's, Dick's, or Carrie's."

"What do I have to say that's so different? I'm not an expert on cutting classes, any more than they are. If I were, I wouldn't be in college now."

"Why not say that in the essay?"

"Say what?"

"That you don't believe in cutting classes. Have you *ever* cut a class?"

"Sure. Last year I cut the first day of hunting season, but I told my teachers and got the assignments."

"Why not say that in the essay? Have you cut here?"

"I cut a history lecture two weeks ago because I had a math hourly the next period. I guess that did not help any, though. It just put me behind in history. And my roommate had even more trouble. He cut the whole third week of the semester, and he's still recovering. I think he was surprised when no truant officer came after him. When he went back he found it almost impossible to catch up, especially in his technical subjects."

"Why not put that in the essay?"

"Who cares about me and my roommate? The essay was supposed to be about mandatory class attendance, not about me and my roommate."

"But your essay ignores your most important and most interesting source of support for such an essay— your own experiences. Let me ask you something else. Do you *really* think that students should be completely free to cut all their classes? Do you think someone *should* have come calling on your roommate to help him avoid failing out?"

"He went back on his own and learned a good lesson about misusing freedom. I was getting a little worried, though. Like, I wondered what would happen if he cut a second and then a third week. That would have meant real trouble. Too many cuts can signal some sort of serious problem, and I suppose *somebody* ought to check things out before a guy flunks."

"Then you think students ought to have only limited freedom to cut classes?"

"Well, ideally, but you said to take a definite stand."

"That is a definite stand."

"Okay. And then you want me to give all these examples about the possible consequences of too much cutting?"

"Sure, along with some examples from your own experience and observation about what you've learned about responsible ways to cut classes."

"I could really write about that."

"About what?"

"Well, you know, about mandatory class attendance not being necessary for students who plan ahead for their cuts and who arrange ahead of time to make up the work they miss."

"Sounds good to me, and much more interesting than that first blob you wrote. Reading that was like trying to punch a pillow. I never connected with anything real or solid."

"Nobody ever called my writing a blob before."

"Let me express the secret of writing as a mathematical formula: $W = A + S$. *Writing* equals *Assertion* plus *Support*. You have given me a few assertions in that essay, but almost no support. Prop up your blob, give it backbone, some stiffness, by giving concrete examples about how you learned to cut a class creatively and responsibly—something your roommate has had to learn the hard way, and almost too late."

"I tried to tell him."

"Did you use examples?"

"Sure. One, anyhow. Of course, he didn't really want to hear too much about what a responsible student I am."

"I want to hear about it, or at least about responsible class cutting, with your own experiences and observations worked in as supporting examples. I want to hear about how you found out about the material in the history lecture you missed. I want to hear about which subjects you feel you can risk taking cuts in, and why. I want to hear about which kinds of teachers don't mind when students cut their classes."

"You want to know all those details? That would be easy to write. I could fill up a whole essay with supporting examples like that."

"That's development!"

CHAPTER 23

FINDING THE RIGHT WORD

> You must remember this:
> A kiss is just a kiss.

These are the opening lyrics of "As Time Goes By," made
popular after Dooley Wilson sang the song in the movie
Casablanca several decades ago. We all know, however,
that kisses are not just kisses. Certainly not all kisses
are alike. Some are wet. Some are dry. Some are short.
Some are long. Some are duty kisses, like those for Aunt
Mabel. Some are caring kisses, like for the widow of
Sammy Brown. Some are passion kisses, like for . . . ,
well, whoever we are feeling passionate about this week.
Some are a way of saying good night. Some are a way of
saying, "Please don't leave yet." Words are like kisses.
No two are quite alike. No two have quite the same
meaning. And just as we learn to distinguish among
the various feelings or messages to be conveyed by a

kiss, so we must learn to distinguish among the various
meanings words can have. If we can do that, then we are
ready to select the words that will permit us to say what
we need to say. Although there are no firm rules about
diction—a fancy term for word selection—we are usually

WORDS ARE LIKE KISSES: NO TWO ARE QUITE ALIKE...

better off if we make sure that our words are as precise, as short, as concrete, and as informal as possible.

You must first choose words that are precise, words that convey to another person the exact meaning you are trying to convey. That is no small task, because words have subtle shades of meaning, and those shades can shift with the context in which the words appear. Few words in context can be fully defined in terms of their denotations or their explicit dictionary meanings alone. Almost all words carry connotations, or implicit meanings, as well. They suggest or call to mind associations beyond their literal meaning. Another little ditty—this one quite sexist—makes this point:

> Call a woman a kitten, but never a cat;
> Call her a mouse, but never a rat;
> Call her a chick, but never a hen;
> Or you surely will not be her caller again.

Do not be fooled into thinking you can substitute one word for another simply because a thesaurus groups them together under a single entry. The thesaurus will do you little good unless you are familiar with the connotations of possible synonyms for a given word. "Portly," "chubby," "chunky," "heavy," "overweight," "stocky," "plump," and "obese" are all possible synonyms for "fat," but they are not interchangeable. "Fat" usually has unpleasant connotations; "obese" is often used in a technical or medical context; "stocky" can mean merely short and muscular; "chunky" is sometimes used to describe young children who still have their "baby fat," which itself is sometimes a prettier term for plain "fat." Your task is to select the word that conveys most accurately the precise shade of meaning or feeling you intend.

Just as your words should be precise, so they should, if you have a choice, generally be short rather than long. Now, there is nothing inherently wrong with big words like "inherently." There are times, however, when we feel inclined to utilize the big word simply because we feel that it somehow makes our writing more impressive. An example is the word "utilize" in the previous sentence. The word "use" would have done the job just as well. Why should we utilize a writing implement when we can use a pencil? Why should we terminate a class when we can end it? Why should we transmit a letter when we can send it? Why should we osculate when we can kiss? Why should we speak of the temporary nonavailability of automotive leasing units when what we mean is that all the cars have been rented? Why should we find the engine inoperative subsequent to the period of inclement weather when all we mean is that we cannot start the damned car after the snowstorm? Poets for centuries have enjoyed the poetic richness of the English language because it allows them to draw from Germanic, French, and Latin word stocks. Shakespeare, for example, spoke of "incarnadining" the seas, then quickly explained that what he meant was making them red with blood. You are usually better off in your own writing to make red than to incarnadine. Your readers may not be so impressed with your fancy vocabulary, but they will know what you are trying to say. It is far more important that they know what you mean than that they be impressed with your ability to obfuscate by utilizing elongated terminological constructions.

Just as you are almost always better off selecting a short word than a long one of comparable meaning, so you are almost always better off selecting a concrete word or phrase than an abstract one. A "fastening device" is more abstract than a "nail" or "screw" or "bolt" or "wire" or "tape." Tape is more abstract than "a piece of masking tape six inches long" or "a roll of double-stick cellophane tape." You can tell your readers that "a thief robbed me" and leave it at that. But if that is all you say, your readers will have little idea of what happened. If you tell your readers that "a man took my money," they will know a little more. But you can do even better. Instead of "a man," how about "a stocky man of about twenty, wearing a purple Miami sweatshirt and a yellow ski mask"? Instead of "money," how about "$175"? Whether you are writing a police report, an insurance claim, or a college essay about the need for better security on campus, it is obvious how much more effective the concrete words are than the abstract "a thief robbed me." There may be occasions, of course, when the more abstract expression is what you are after, but just now I cannot think of such an occasion. If it is important to tell your readers that you were robbed, it is almost certainly important that they know something about who the thief was and what the thief took from you. Before I go on to the next chapter, where

I shall have more to say about concreteness, I want to
say a word about informal diction.

   Just as you must choose between precise and
imprecise words, between long and short words,
between concrete and abstract words, so you must
decide between formal and informal words. Formal
words, like formal clothing, have their place. There
may be times when the formal "institution of higher
learning" will be what you want to refer to, but most
of the time the more informal "college" will do just
fine. There may be times when you want to refer to
"apartments shared by men and women," but usually
"coed apartments" is better. Of course, writing can
easily become too informal. Your college can become
"hey, man, ya know, this monkey cage," and your
apartment can become "the slime pit" or some other
private slang expression. Unless your purpose in the
essay you are writing is to show why college is like a
monkey cage or why you think of your apartment as
a slime pit, you are generally better off avoiding the
extremes of trendy or slang expressions. While you want
to avoid sounding too learned or snobbish, you also want
to avoid sounding too moronic or slovenly by trying to
write street jargon. Select colorful, specific, functional
words, somewhere between what you might feel inclined
to use in a job interview and what you might use in
a discussion over hamburgers with three of your old
high school friends. Informal diction offers variety and
versatility, and certainly it is easier and more enjoyable
to read and to understand. For these reasons it has

become the preferred mode in modern English, even in serious writing on significant subjects for sophisticated audiences.

Mark Twain once said, "The difference between the right and the almost right word is the difference between lightning and the lightning bug." If you want to write lightning essays, or even just plain enlightening ones, you should use precise, short, concrete, and informal words. Strike your reader with lightning. What reader wants to be kissed by a lightning bug?

CHAPTER 24

WRITING CONCRETELY

Pretend for a moment, since this would never *really* happen to you, that you are struggling in an 8 a.m. English class to maintain some appearance of consciousness while your professor drones on about Ezra Pound's theory of images and abstractions. Suddenly you hear a loud explosion from somewhere down the hall, followed by the clamor of hurried footsteps and excited voices. The professor runs out to take a look, then returns and continues to drone on about Pound. Now wide awake, you are desperate to discover the cause of the commotion. "What was that?" you blurt out. "A noise," your professor answers. "What's all that commotion?" "Voices," he calmly responds. If the "noise" and the "voices" continue much longer, you will probably leap from your seat, throttle the professor, and fling open the door. What causes your frustration is the refusal of your professor, your source of information, to provide anything more than general and abstract answers. What makes you want to strangle him until his eyes pop is his refusal to give you *details*.

The same frustration can occur for a reader. Think of the professor as a writer, your source of information. And think of yourself, the student, as a reader. You become angry because your writer supplies no concrete language to *show* you, since you cannot see through the door, the event outside. You would have been much more satisfied had the professor described the scene: "There is smoke and dust pouring from the washroom. Seven English professors are wrestling with a dust-covered young man named Wilson Plunkett, who just blew up the men's rest room after screaming something about his first failing grade ever on an English paper." Such a response would satisfy your curiosity, at least somewhat. Perhaps it would even elicit a roar of approval and applause from most of the class. Concrete writing does the same thing. It satisfies curiosity and gives the reader something to react to, something to see, hear, touch, smell, and taste, or something to applaud. Concrete writing involves the reader in the writing. It forces the reader to consider more carefully the writer's views, and it makes the writer more interesting, more satisfying, and more lively than the dullard who responds, "noise," "voices."

We all hate to be bored, and we are all naturally curious. We slow down and look when we pass automobile accidents. We listen intently to gossip. We demand more and more newspaper articles and television shows about the private lives of movie stars and politicians. We are curious even in our reading. We demand to know. Consider the following sentences taken from student essays:

> "I walked pretty far in bad weather to get to her home."

> "I had a good job this summer."

> "She does not like good music."

> "He offered some advice on the handling of my roommate."

> "We established a good, healthy relationship."

We want to scream, after each of these sentences, "How?" "What?" "Who?" If we could, we would throttle the writer and fling open the door. On the other side we might find:

> "I trudged four miles through the rain to get to her mansion on Elderberry Hill."

> "This summer I had a job making corn dogs at the Jersey shore; I earned $2,300, got a deep tan, and fell in love twice."

> "Mary, unfortunately, refuses to listen to anything by the Grateful Dead."

> "On the care and feeding of my roommate, my resident assistant suggested I hire Wilson Plunkett, the student who blew up the English Department men's room last semester."

```
"My girlfriend now does my laundry
for me."
```

Most of our "how's," "what's," and "who's" have been
answered in the second set of sentences. The writing in
the second set is more interesting, lively, and clear. We
can see what the writer sees.

Getting readers to see what the writer sees is one of
the writer's hardest jobs, but concrete writing makes the
job much easier. Writing concretely ensures that writers
are not misunderstood, that their points are not altered
by readers abandoned to interpret the writing any way
they want. For example, suppose someone wrote, "My
car is at my mother's house." Readers left to their own
devices might imagine a fire-engine red '71 'Cuda, 383,
V-8 with a Shaker hood scoop and chrome tailpipe tips
parked in the driveway of a pink-shingled white home
in a suburban development in Roslyn, Long Island.
The writer's car, however, is a '74 Ford, part rust, part
bondo and primer paint, balanced precariously on cinder
blocks in the front yard of a weather-beaten bungalow
in western Ohio. Of course, the writer's purpose might
not be to go on and on describing her car, but she stands
a lesser chance of being misunderstood if she speaks
concretely, if she says "'74 Ford" instead of "car," if she
says "seven English professors wrestling a dust-covered
young man" instead of "noise."

The greatest pitfall of writing abstractly is not,
however, the danger of being misunderstood; it is
the danger of being meaningless. Writers who use
concrete language avoid the abyss they fall into when
they write "enjoyable experience," "nice atmosphere,"

"interesting environment," or, even worse, phrases like "the American way of life." Such phrases have no consistent meaning for readers. Concrete writing means something: "My first camping trip showed me that I had spent too many hours of my life drawing nourishment, like a house plant, from fluorescent light"; "No one spoke above a whisper in the candle-lit restaurant"; "His office was cluttered with paper, books, coffee mugs, and sweaters; yet nothing looked out of place, except him"; "In America, we can now buy what we have been craving for decades—a thumb-operated pocket phone that lets us use a satellite to find the nearest pizza joint and then photograph the greasy chef spinning a wad of dough."

In the words of Ezra Pound, "Go in fear of abstractions." Class dismissed.

CHAPTER 25

MEPHOBIA:
AN EYE FOR A EWE

A subtle form of rot has crept into the writing of many American students. I call this rot mephobia (pronounced "mee-FOE-bee-ah"). And because I invented the word I get to define it. Mephobia is the fear of mentioning oneself in writing. Sometimes this phobia grows from English or journalism teachers who tell their students, "Never use the first person." Sometimes it grows from modesty, a feeling that no one really wants to know about plain little old me. Sometimes it grows from a worship of science, in which absolute objectivity is the desired goal, whereas no mere human can be absolutely objective. Sometimes it grows from ideals of democracy, in which the importance of the majority is supposed to take precedence over the importance of the individual. Sometimes it grows from simple cowardice, which

causes a writer to fear standing up and stating an
opinion in his or her own voice. Whatever the source of
mephobia, however, it is an ugly cancer on our writing
and must be cut out. I have isolated two kinds of
mephobia: grand mephobia and petit mephobia. Grand
mephobia is seen in writers who always, if given a
chance, choose to write on topics like "America's foreign
policy" or "The need for a balanced budget" rather than
"On being the only African-American in class" or "The
trouble with Thanksgiving vacation." I will say no
more about grand mephobia except that students who
are perennially afraid to deal with their own lives and
experiences are seriously ill. Petit mephobia, on the
other hand, affects even healthy writers who are willing
to write about their own experiences. Petit mephobia
has several easily recognized symptoms and is relatively
easy to cure.

One symptom of mephobia is the use of awkward
phrases like "the present writer." Patients use this silly
phrase not because they want to make a distinction
between a present writer and one who is either absent
or who lived in the past. It is, rather, that they are
afraid to write those dreaded little pronouns "I,"
"me," "we," and "us." They say, "The present writer is
inclined to the belief that William Faulkner is a more
enduring American writer than Ernest Hemingway"
when what they ought to be saying is a simple, "I
think Faulkner will be with us long after America has
forgotten Hemingway." They have us read, "The present
investigators, while aware of the need for further study
before firm conclusions can be drawn, lean toward the

belief that a cure for the common cold will continue to elude science for a minimal period of time of at least two more decades" when what they ought to give us to read is a simple, "Dr. Cutty and I do not think we will see a cure for the common cold in the next twenty years."

A more pernicious symptom of mephobia is the use of the passive voice. In this poor excuse for bold writing, patients refuse to name any doer or thinker at all, not even "the present writer." Patients with this symptom try our patience with tripe like this:

> The party was held in the Taylor Red
> Lounge between 9 p.m. and midnight.
> Cider and pretzels were served. There
> was no live band, but records and tapes
> were played. Even though it was a quiet
> party, a good time was had by all who
> attended.

To me that sounds like a lifeless, boring, ghostly party, with all those things being done and no one doing them. How much better it sounds if there are some doers:

> The literary club threw a party in
> the Taylor Red Lounge last Saturday. We
> started around nine, and by midnight Sam
> was silly from the rancid cider and Jill
> was bloated from the pretzels. I played
> my favorite records and tapes until I
> was removed for showing favoritism for
> the Beatles and Elvis Presley. Then
> Shirley got things quieted down with her
> "I'm Dreaming of a White Christmas,"
> which got us all acting goofy because
> Christmas is, after all, two months
> away. At midnight we all sang "Jingle

Bells" and, grinning like idiots, went
home.

The good news is that most beginning writers
manage to avoid the "present writer" syndrome and
fortunately seem to recoil instinctively from the
pernicious passive voice. The bad news is that many
do not seem to have an innate sense about the quietest
symptom of mephobia, the use of "you" instead of
"I." In essay after essay I read this kind of awkward
indirection:

> When you walk into that first calculus
> lecture you look cautiously around the
> room for your roommate. Your heart sinks
> when you see that he is not there. You
> take a seat among all those strangers
> and wait, cringing, until the professor
> walks in. She looks around the room as
> if you are all figures on the wallpaper.
> Then she reads your names off a computer
> list and mispronounces yours, when she
> comes to it. All in all, you wind up
> feeling like a snowflake on a glacier.

Who is this "you" we read about? It is not me, because
I am a teacher and I am not taking calculus. It is not
the other students in the English class because none
of them are in that calculus class and many are not
taking calculus at all. No, "you" is not us. "You" is the
writer. But why is he afraid to tell us about his feelings
and experiences? Why is he afraid to do what comes
naturally when talking about his own experiences? The
first person is so much more refreshing:

SAY ALL THAT AND THEN GO FORTH AND WRITE...

When I walked into my first calculus
class the first thing I did was look
cautiously around the room to see
if Ron, my roommate, was there. He
was not. Disappointed, I took a
seat beside the south column. I was
surrounded by strangers. Then the
professor came in. She looked around
the room at us as if we were all
chickens in a packing crate waiting

```
to be driven off to market. She
started reading off the names from
her computer list. When she got to my
name, she of course mispronounced it
"Crone" instead of "Shrone." In the
first fifteen minutes of my first college
class, then, I felt like a pebble in a
glacier, ready to be ground into fine
sand.
```

The revised paragraph, of course, is better in part because the language is more lively and specific, but some of that liveliness and specificity derives from the writer's willingness to refer to himself directly as "I" rather than as "you." There are times, of course, when "you" is all right. When giving directions or advice, for example, there is a place for the second person. In such situations, however, the "you" does not substitute for "I" but is used in conjunction with it. In giving *you* advice on how to write an essay *I* have kept, not fearfully submerged, my own voice.

If you have mephobia you write deadened prose, but you can be cured. All you have to do is find a mirror just before you sit down to write an essay, look yourself in the eye, and say, "Hi, I am me. I am not a present writer. I am not an invisible nameless ghost by whom things are passively done or felt or believed. I am not a you, a ewe, a female sheep. I am an I, an eye, a bold seer. I see. I do. I feel. I believe." Say all that to yourself and then go forth and write a lively, first-person essay. You can do it. I know you can.

CHAPTER 26

MOVING OUT

If this book -has been successful, you will soon outgrow it. If you have learned to apply most of the principles I have discussed, and if you have learned how to imitate the structures of the little essays through which I have presented them, you are ready to move out. The best writers begin to generate their own principles of good writing. They stop imitating models early on. They learn to trust their own instincts about what works in writing. They learn to let the structure of an argument emerge from their evidence rather than trying to impose a structure on their evidence. They learn to sense their readers' state of mind and to know when they can profitably take certain risks.

But I hope that you do not outgrow this book altogether. The principles I have been setting down are, after all, more or less universally accepted. Arguments that are not bold, clear, and well developed will for a long time to come be viewed as cowardly, muddled, and incomplete. Arguments that lack unity, cohesion, and organization will for a long time to come be viewed as wandering, disconnected, and chaotic.

If you have mastered these principles, then you will find yourself making good use of them in many different kinds of writing. Though you may not be writing many "college essays" after you graduate, it is almost certain that you will write arguments in your technical reports, your business letters, your grant proposals, your letters to the editor, and your annual reports. Some of you may become professional writers and publish articles and books. In that postcollege writing your transitions may be less obvious, your skeletal structures less bony, your main points more subtly stated, but the principles you have learned will still stand.

Learning to write is like learning to ride a bike. To ride a bike you need to master a few basic principles of steering, balance, leaning into curves, pedaling, braking, and avoiding potholes and mud puddles. Once you have learned those principles, however, you are ready to move out. You will find that writing is never an all-downhill trip. You will learn that you usually have to work hard to get anywhere. There will be times when you wish you were in a taxi, sitting back and letting someone else drive. But if you stick with your bike and keep in mind the simple principles of riding, you will be amazed at some of the remote paths you can travel and the exotic destinations you can explore.

STUDENT ESSAYS FOR DISCUSSION

The four essays presented in this section were all hand-written during the second class of a first-year college writing course at Lehigh University. I made the assignment as a diagnostic tool because I wanted to see what kind of writing my students did "naturally," before I had taught them anything about how to write. I was also interested in what they had to say about the topic "Effective Teachers." My only instructions were that the students were to write an essay, based on their own personal experience in high school, in which they made and supported a point about teachers.

After class I read through all of the essays and selected these four for class discussion. As I typed these essays from the students' handwritten essays, I corrected spelling errors, fixed some obvious errors in punctuation, and altered the names of the specific teachers identified. Otherwise, however, I present the essays just as the students wrote them.

At the start of the following class period I
distributed these essays, anonymously of course, and
asked the students to read them quickly and rank-order
them according to whatever principles of good writing
they wanted to apply. I tallied their ratings on the
blackboard. We then discussed why they liked the two
that received the highest ratings. You might want to do
a similar rating in your class, using either these essays
or ones you and your classmates have written.

1. The Wrong Way to Teach

My eleventh-grade United States history
teacher had the worst combination of teaching
methods and personality traits that a teacher
could possibly have. She was unorganized and
random, making it impossible to follow her
teaching, but that didn't matter because
your grade depended mainly upon her personal
feelings for you and whether or not she
agreed with your opinions.

In every history class I have taken,
history was chronological. However, Mrs.
McDougal had some other order of historical
events committed to memory. She made it
nearly impossible to keep up with her
teaching because she jumped from one era to
another quite randomly. The class was left
in utter confusion, wondering how we moved
from Franklin D. Roosevelt to the Industrial
Revolution.

During every lecture, she would come
to some profound conclusion that only she
understood, explaining with her favorite

phrase, "It's deja vu all over again." Of course, most of the class had missed the half-second in which we had covered this amazing insight. Assignments were frequent, especially essays. However, she rarely followed through enough to collect them, and the grades were even more uncommon. The threat of a test or a quiz came at least once a week, but the total taken was actually two or three. I still do not know how she justified the grades she handed out.

Mrs. McDougal did literally hand out grades. If I had been judged on the amount of work I did, I would have failed the class. However, I was one of the chosen few. She called me her friend. She preferred to have personal conversations rather than answer my history questions. I never even wrote my first semester term paper. I discussed the topic with her, instead. Of course, none of the other students were supposed to know about that. There were other chosen ones. Jason Higgins was her gopher. He organized her bookshelves and papers. He always agreed with her. As far as she was concerned, he could do no wrong. She liked him so much that she tried to find him a date for the prom. Our grades reflected these personal relations. While I am glad that I passed the class for the sake of my grade-point average, I learned next to nothing that year. I received a 2 on the Advanced Placement test. I would much rather have had a teacher who cared about what I was learning more than my personal life. I might have failed, but I would have learned at least one lesson.

2. Bad Teaching and the R easons for It

There are many different kinds of
teachers, and usually one is exposed to both
the good and the bad throughout the course
of their education. From experience, though,
I have found bad teaching occurs when an
instructor fails to listen, does not provide
an atmosphere for "thinking" or "learning,"
and is not enthusiastic about the course he
or she is teaching. Most of the time, if
one of these things is present in a course,
a student not only becomes frustrated and
uninterested, but also is prone to feel
spiteful towards the instructor and ends up
hurting themselves because of it.

A failure to listen to the students in
his or her class is usually found in teachers
who insist upon lecturing as opposed to
teaching. A teacher I had in high school,
Mr. Finbark, was this way. He insisted on
putting ideas into our heads and not being
open to our opinions and questions. To most
of us it seemed that he did not care for the
individuals in his class. The only thing that
mattered to him was that the whole group
got his message and thus thought the same.
There were even times when the tension would
build up so much in class that either he or a
student would "explode." It is not possible
to enjoy or get anything out of a class that
is conducted in this manner.

Also not present in Mr. Finbark's
class was a suitable atmosphere for learning
or thinking. By simply implanting his
thoughts into our minds, we did not have

an opportunity to develop our own ideas or
opinions. This class was simply a three-
step process consisting of lecturing,
memorization, and regurgitation. And,
truthfully, you could add a fourth step
which would be forgetting the material. If
I dug deep, I could probably tell you one
or two of the main points from the class,
but that is about it. I did not "learn"
anything from the class because there was no
thinking involved. I also found this to be
true in my world history class where I had
Mr. Westony. In this class we were expected
to memorize dates and events, but once again
there was no individual thinking involved.
On the other hand, the next year I took an
American history course with Dr. Manypacker.
On the first day of class he defined history as
"interpretation." This definition paved the
way for a class which was both worthwhile and
enjoyable. Because I was interested in the
class, I was able to learn more in the class,
and consequently get more out of it than
simply a good grade.

   The third thing which brings about bad
teaching is an instructor who simply doesn't
enjoy what he or she is doing. It may be a
teacher who is forced to teach a beginning
course or, as was the case in my high school,
a coach who had to teach a history course.
Mr. Canfeld was the varsity football coach
but, according to school rules, he had to
teach an academic course in the school.
It was evident from the first day that he
didn't want to be there and this not only
put a damper on our spirits and enthusiasm,

but also made learning anything impossible.
Contrastingly, I had a senior year calculus
course with Mr. Bacon. Going in, I knew it
would be tough and expected to simply abhor
going to class and doing the work, but in the
end I realized that it was one of the best
courses I had ever taken and probably would
be one of the best ever. He had an enthusiasm
for math that went beyond classroom work and
included advising and special sessions for
application work and studying. If you can find
a teacher like this it will truly be a very
worthwhile experience.

It is a real shame that there are so
many bad teachers in our world today. It is
my opinion that any course can be interesting
and informative if it is taught in the right
way. This includes listening to and caring
for the students, encouraging them to think
for themselves, and showing them you enjoy
what you are doing.

3. Those Few Good Teachers

I believe that the most effective
teachers are those who have sincere
enthusiasm for what they are doing. This
enthusiasm is demonstrated by their work
outside class, as well as being seen directly
in the classroom.

Teachers who are truly enthusiastic
about their class will take the time and
energy to fully prepare for the class.
The teachers will search for the best way
to present the material. Lesson plans are

organized and often contain an original
way to conduct class. For example, my math
teacher in high school always gave extremely
organized notes. The order in which she gave
them made them easier to understand. Also, as
math is often a lecture-only class, she would
develop projects to break up the monotony of
regular classes.

Enthusiastic teachers will also take
time outside of class to work with students.
Their enthusiasm is responsible for not only
making themselves available, but also for
drawing their students in for help. Extra
help outside of class, often after school, is
never a place students want to go. However,
with an enthusiastic teacher, the prospect is
much more inviting. Again, my math teacher's
enthusiasm made me much more likely to go
for extra help when I needed it. However,
teachers' enthusiasm inside the classroom
may be their greatest asset. They act more
as if they were talking about something they
enjoy, rather than teaching a subject. It is
as if they are carrying on a conversation
with their students. Therefore, they do not
drone on endlessly, but break midway through
facts to offer comments. They speak with an
upbeat voice, which definitely has a large
effect on the effectiveness of the class.
Enthusiastic teachers usually allow students
to participate in class, answering questions
and offering their own comments. This can
happen even in structured classes such as
math, but is even easier in a seminar-
style class such as English. I had two very
effective, very enthusiastic English teachers

in high school. Both treated class as a discussion among a group of people, not as an adult teaching children. I learned so much more by discussing, rather than being told.

Probably the largest reason that an enthusiastic teacher is most effective is that they cause students to be enthusiastic also. Students begin to see the subject through the teachers' eyes. They begin to see the value of the material, as well as the enjoyment it can bring. I believe that it is almost impossible to not enjoy something or at least respect something when someone else enjoys it so much. I already liked math and English, but my enthusiastic teachers caused me to like them even more. But I believe the best example was my Advanced Placement English class. At the beginning of the year, almost all the students in the class hated reading poems. However, our teacher would get so excited and so moved by them that we all had to laugh at her enthusiasm, and most of us ended up enjoying the poems, too. I guess that enthusiasm is just contagious.

4. A Teacher Who Cared

When I was a freshman in high school, I failed integrated math. Last year, as a senior, I earned an A in calculus and scored a 5 (a perfect score) on the Advanced Placement exam. You may ask, "Why was there such a difference in your performance?" No, I didn't take any intelligence-enhancing drugs. I just got a new teacher. This teacher was everything an excellent teacher should be; he

was caring, creative, and impassioned about
what he taught.

    My freshman teacher, Mrs. Harringbone,
was a prime example of how not to teach. If
a student didn't understand something, they
had to find their own tutor to explain the
material. She was too busy teaching to make
sure her students learned. She was impatient
with imperfection, and anything not done her
way was wrong.

    Kooz, my A.P. calculus teacher, arranged
individual time with students to tutor them.
If a student didn't understand something,
Kooz took it upon himself to make sure they
did. He realized that everyone learned in a
different manner and at a different pace. He
allowed for this and gave confidence to each
of his students.

    Kooz believed I could do anything. Mrs.
Harringbone believed that I would never be
good enough. The first day of class, she told
us that she didn't expect the girls to do as
well as the boys, because girls are not good
at math. The first day of A.P. calculus, Kooz
said that anyone could get an A in calculus.
I lived up to both their expectations. A good
teacher always believes in their students.

    Caring about the students is not enough.
A good teacher must be excited and interested
in the material they teach. Mrs. Harringbone
did not like our textbook, and she never
hesitated to let us know. She thought the
information was oversimplified. Even with
oversimplified information, I failed. My
teacher did not believe in me or in what she
taught.

On the other hand, Kooz thought calculus was amazing. He loved how calculus worked, how it was so useful, so simple. All of his students shared a wonder at the language of calculus. We were excited to learn.

In order for a student to learn, the teacher must be innovative in conveying the materials. Nobody wants to be talked at an hour a day, five days a week. It's hard to pay attention to a dry lecture. If a teacher is creative and varied in their methods of teaching, the students will be more excited about going to class, and they will find it easier to focus when they get there.

As a freshman in high school, I fell asleep in math once or twice a week. I made every effort not to: I brought cups of coffee, I took diligent notes, I pinched myself when I began to doze off. The only way I could stay awake was to ignore the teacher and talk to my friend. Either way, I learned almost nothing.

I had Kooz two years in a row: my junior year at 7:30 in the morning, and my senior year right after lunch. I never fell asleep. Kooz was engaging and fun. He had the students participate in the class by solving problems on the board, by explaining what we knew to other students, by creating games to test our skills, and by answering specific questions. Kooz told jokes, but everybody in that class understood almost everything on those tests.

The teacher makes all the difference. With the "oversimplified" information I was taught freshman year, 60% of my class failed.

In the A.P. class I took senior year, nobody failed, and 75% of the class earned A's. Some of these students were the same ones who had failed integrated math with me.

The different was not just the teaching style. Where Mrs. Harringbone was indifferent, Kooz cared. When Mrs. Harringbone was pessimistic, Kooz believed. When Mrs. Harringbone talked at us, Kooz listened when we talked back. Kooz did not just spout information; he taught.

I learned because my teacher was creative, interested in what he taught, and he cared. No matter how bright a student is, they cannot learn without being taught. The most successful teachers are the ones who learn and grow right along with their students.

EDITING MATTERS

Way back in my chapter on "What Is an Acceptable Essay?" I said, almost in passing, that an acceptable essay presupposes the ability of the writer to "use proper grammar and decently constructed sentences." I did not say much more about grammar and sentences at the time. Indeed, many college writing teachers do not talk much about grammar or other mechanical features of writing in class, because many college writers make few mistakes in grammar, usage, spelling, syntax, or citation. Still, they make some mistakes, and it is irresponsible for either the teacher or the student to ignore them. In this section of my book I describe certain problems that I have found over the years tend to occur and reoccur in student papers. Listed here are some of the most important of those problems. Your instructor may want to use the numbers in the margins of your papers to indicate words, phrases, or sentences that need your attention. The more esoteric errors your instructor will correct for you or show you in some other way how to correct. Of course, we all know that most rules about writing can be effectively broken by good writers. Until you gain experience and self-confidence, however, you will do well to heed these helpful hints.

1. **FRAGMENT.** A sentence fragment occurs when a group of words lacks a subject or predicate or when a clause—a group of words with a subject and verb—is dependent on a separated group of words for its meaning. To correct a fragment, either insert the subject or verb, or complete the idea of the dependent clause by joining it with an independent one.

> *Faulty:* Life in New York is dangerous to your health. Particularly if you are wearing a gold chain.
>
> Running naked across the bridge.

> *Better:* Life in New York is dangerous to your health, particularly if you are wearing a gold chain.
>
> He ran naked across the bridge.

2. **COMMA SPLICE.** A comma splice occurs when two sentences are incorrectly joined using a comma without a coordinating conjunction such as "and," "but," "or," "so," "for," or "yet." Note that "however," "therefore," and "thus" are conjunctive adverbs, not coordinating conjunctions. Do not worry about the weird terminology that grammarians use, but do avoid thinking, for example, that "but" and "however" are synonyms, or that "so" and "thus" are. This kind of thinking leads to comma splices. There

are various ways to correct a comma splice. You
can insert a coordinating conjunction, replace the
comma with a period or a semicolon, or add words to
indicate the relationship between the two sentences.

Faulty: I went to the library, I fell
        asleep.

Better: I went to the library, but I fell
        asleep.

        I went to the library. I fell
        asleep.

        I went to the library, where I fell
        asleep.

3. **FUSED SENTENCES.** Two sentences jammed
   together with no punctuation are said to be fused.
   There are several ways to defuse such errors. The
   simplest is to separate the two parts into individual
   sentences. You can also subordinate one sentence
   to the other or combine the two ideas in some other
   way.

Faulty: I arrived at the University Center
        late for dinner I got a platter of
        mystery meat anyway.

Better: I arrived at the University Center
        late for dinner. I got a platter of
        mystery meat anyway.

        Although I arrived at the
        University Center late for dinner,
        I got a platter of mystery meat.

```
Arriving late at the University
Center for dinner, I begged a
platter of mystery meat.
```

4. **TENSE SHIFT.** Tense shift occurs when writers change from one tense to another but do not intend to indicate a difference in time. To correct an unnecessary tense shift, maintain a uniform tense within a sentence or entire essay unless you intend to indicate a change in time.

Faulty: When semester break approaches, the residence halls emptied quickly.

Better: When semester break approaches, the residence halls empty quickly.

Some writers have trouble knowing what tense to use when they write about literature and, in their uncertainty, shift tenses. It is quite all right to use the present tense when dealing with literature: "Alison is probably the worst sinner of them all. She uses . . . ." But above all, do not change tense unless you mean to indicate a change in time: "Alison, even though she had married an unattractive husband, is probably the worst sinner of them all."

5. **FAULTY SUBJECT-VERB AGREEMENT.** A verb must agree with its subject. A problem occurs when a singular verb follows a plural noun, or vice versa. To correct the problem, either change the subject or, preferably, the verb, so that the two agree.

Faulty: She don't like me.

The pleasures of a cook includes eating the meal.

Better: She doesn't like me.

The pleasures of a cook include eating the meal.

Be particularly careful when the subject is at some distance from the v erb it controls.

Faulty: The headlights of the 1978 Cadillac at the back of the parking lot was smashed in.

The highway through the mountains run all the way to the border.

The laughter of the presidential candidates have helped us all to see the triviality of the "save-the-salamanders" issue.

Better: The headlights of the 1978 Cadillac at the back of the parking lot were smashed in.

The highway through the mountains runs all the way to the border.

The laughter of the presidential candidates has helped us all to see the triviality of the "save-the-salanders" issue.

Watch out for nouns that look plural but that are usually treated as singular and so require a singular verb form: "mathematics," "politics," "athletics," "measles," "news," "economics," and so on. Similarly, collective nouns like "crowd," "class," "family," and "committee" are—at least in American English—treated as singular even though they comprise several members.

Faulty: Politics keep the nation from fixing its economic problems.

The news this morning are most troubling.

The jury are now in deliberation.

My class are out at Mr. Noodle's Bistro eating lunch.

Better: Politics keeps the nation from fixing its economic problems.

The news this morning is most troubling.

The jury is now in deliberation.

My class is out at Mr. Noodle's Bistro eating lunch.

Dual subjects joined by "and" generally take a plural verb form. For dual subjects joined by "or" or "nor," the verb generally agrees with the subject element that is closest to it.

Faulty: Huckleberry Finn and his father likes living away from civilization.

If a Chinese or a Japanese woman show up in the emergency ward, it is safest to call for an interpreter immediately.

```
Neither the professor nor his
students was able to figure out how
to turn the air conditioner on.
```

Better: Huckleberry Finn and his father
like living away from civilization.

If a Chinese or a Japanese woman
shows up in the emergency ward,
it is safest to call for an
interpreter immediately.

Neither the professor nor his
students were able to figure out how
to turn the air conditioner on.

6. FAULTY PRONOUN-ANTECEDENT AGREEMENT.

A pronoun must agree in number with its antecedent. A problem occurs when a singular pronoun is made to refer to a plural noun, or vice versa. Sometimes faulty agreement results when a writer tries to avoid sexist language in their sentences. In that last sentence, I created an error by using "their" to avoid using "his" to refer to both men and women writers. Often the best solution is to switch to a plural subject.

Faulty: Everyone did his best on the exam.

Better: All of the students did their best
on the exam.

We all did our best on the exam.

Be careful if you conjoin a pronoun with a noun or another pronoun. In such compounds try saying the sentence without the first word in the compound.

Since you would not say "the counselor gave myself," "me was told," "the dean told I to call," or "me went to town," why use such constructions when you add another person?

Faulty: The marriage counselor gave my husband and myself some good advice on how to argue positively.

The contest winners, Mary and me, were told to come forward to the judges' circle together.

The dean of students told Sam and I to call our parents immediately.

Me and her went to town on our bicycles.

Better: The marriage counselor gave my husband and me some good advice on how to argue positively.

The contest winners, Mary and I, were told to come forward to the judges' circle together.

The dean of students told Sam and me to call our parents immediately.

She and I went to town on our bicycles.

7. AMBIGUOUS PRONOUN REFERENCE.

Pronoun reference becomes a problem when the antecedent—the noun the pronoun represents—is unclear to readers. To correct ambiguous pronoun reference, change the word order in some way or simply repeat the noun.

Faulty: My roommate smokes cigars, eats
cashew nuts twenty-four hours a
day, and plays loud Bon Jovi tapes
at 4 a.m. They drive me crazy.

Better: My roommate smokes cigars, eats
cashew nuts twenty-four hours a
day, and plays loud Bon Jovi tapes
at 4 a.m. Her habits drive me
crazy.

8. SHIFT IN PERSON. "Person" reflects the point
of view in which a piece of writing is composed: "I,"
"you," "they," and so on. Good writing is consistent
in its use of one point of view, unless the subject
changes.

Faulty: The fraternities were competing
for recognition in community
service. Sig Ep gave a party for
the Headstart kids on Saturday
and started a food bank for needy
families. You really had to work
hard to be a brother in that
fraternity.

Better: The fraternities were competing
for recognition in community
service. Sig Ep gave a party for
the Headstart kids on Saturday
and started a food bank for needy
families. The fraternity brothers
really had to work hard.

9. DANGLING MODIFERS. A dangling modifier
incorrectly seems to modify a nearby word before
which it "dangles." Most dangling modifiers occur at

the beginning of sentences and appear to replace the true subject of the sentence. To correct this problem, either change the opening phrase or add the correct subject.

Faulty: Walking across campus on a Sunday morning, the campus seemed deserted.

Better: Walking across campus on a Sunday morning, I noticed that the campus seemed deserted.

On my Sunday morning walk, I noticed that the campus seemed deserted.

10. **PASSIVE VOICE.** The voice of a verb shows whether the subject performs or receives the action the verb expresses. A verb is active when the subject performs the action ("The cat ate the mouse."), but passive when the subject is acted upon by the verb ("The mouse was eaten."). Although there are times when the passive is acceptable—"When we came home we found that the house had been broken into"—it is almost always better to write in the active voice.

Faulty: Adjustments have been made in my life to improve my grades.

Better: I have made adjustments in my life to improve my grades.

11. **SEXIST LANGUAGE.** Good writers are learning to avoid what is sometimes called sexist language.

More than a century ago Thoreau could get away
with writing, "The mass of men lead lives of quiet
desperation." Today he would have to write, "The
mass of people lead lives of quiet desperation,"
unless, of course, he meant to suggest that men
despair more quietly than women—itself a sexist
notion. For most writers sexist language takes the
form of using the male pronoun to refer to both
men and women. Usually switching to the plural is
better.

Faulty: After paying his bill at the
bursar's office, the student will
proceed to the registrar's office,
show his receipt, and pick up his
class schedule.

Better: After paying his or her bill at the
bursar's office, the student will
proceed to the registrar's office,
show the receipt, and pick up the
class schedule.

After paying their bills at the
bursar's office, students will
proceed to the registrar's office,
show their receipts, and pick up
their class schedules.

If you use a plural pronoun to avoid sexist language,
then be sure that you have not inadvertently caused
a shift in number.

Faulty: A listener who wants a chance to
win two free tickets to the Cubs
game should send their name and
address to this station.

> ***Better:*** Listeners who want a chance to win
> two free tickets to the Cubs game
> should send their name and address
> to this station.

12. **CARELESS USE OF "YOU."** Some students
use the pronoun "you" when "I" or "we" or "one" or
"they" or a specific noun would be more appropriate.
Generally avoid the use of "you" in college essays
unless you are giving instructions.

> ***Faulty:*** When you first arrive on campus,
> you notice the beauty of the
> architecture.

> ***Better:*** When visitors first arrive on
> campus, they notice the beauty of
> the architecture.
>
> The first time I visited the campus
> I noticed the bold gothic stonework
> on the chapel and the contrasting
> modern brick-and-glass library
> right next door.

13. **VAGUE USE OF "THIS."** Using the word "this"
alone, especially at the beginning of a sentence,
is often confusing to readers because they cannot
pinpoint exactly what "this" refers to. To avoid this,
add a specific word or group of words to describe
the concept you have in mind. As you can see, in
that last sentence, "this problem" or, better, "such
confusion" would be a decided improvement over
"this" alone.

Faulty: Peer criticism has become a valuable part of many composition programs. This allows the students to learn more about their own writing. This is very beneficial and often results in improved writing for the entire class.

Better: Peer criticism has become a valuable part of many composition programs. Criticizing each other's work allows the students to learn more about their own writing. This learning process often results in improved writing for the entire class.

14. **MISUSE OF "WHO" AND "WHOM."** The rules are gradually becoming more relaxed, but generally "who" is used as the subject of a verb whereas "whom" is used as the object of a verb or preposition.

Faulty: Who were you speaking of? Whom is the director of the play?

The student who we accepted was born in Havana.

Better: Whom were you speaking of? Who is the director of the play?

The student whom we accepted was born in Havana.

15. **MISUSE OF "WHICH" AND "THAT."** In general, if you can substitute "that" for "which" and still have the sentence make sense, do so.

Faulty: The dog which ate the spoiled
hamburger got sick.

Yoko wrote the song which made her
famous.

Better: The dog that ate the spoiled
hamburger got sick.

Yoko wrote the song that made her
famous.

Note, however, that some writers misuse "that" in situations where "who" would be better. Thus, "The singer that wrote the song became famous" should be, "The singer who wrote the song became famous."

16. **MISUSE OF "HOWEVER."** Although it is sometimes acceptable to begin a sentence with the coordinating conjunction "but," the conjunctive adverb "however" is usually best placed inside the sentence after an opening phrase. If it appears as the first word it may misleadingly appear to be a simple adverb. For example: "But he tried to shoot himself" is acceptable; "However he tried to shoot himself" is less so, because it misleads the reader into thinking that "however" is an adverb modifying "tried," as in the sentence "However he tried to shoot himself he failed, because he did not know how to pull the trigger."

Faulty: The computer program looked
complicated. However, the basic
premise was simple.

Better: The computer program looked
         complicated. The basic premise,
         however, was simple.

         The computer program looked
         complicated, but the basic premise
         was simple.

17. **MISUSE OF "HOPEFULLY."** "Hopefully" means
"in a hopeful manner" or "with hope." It does not
mean "I hope," though an increasing number of
writers use it to mean that. In some circles the
word has achieved acceptance as an alternative to
"I hope," but there are enough purists left that you
would be better not to use it to mean that in formal
writing. I advise you to refuse to place "hopefully" at
the beginning of a sentence. "Hopefully" at the start
of a sentence modifies the verb that follows it. Thus,
"Hopefully he will kiss me" means that "He will kiss
me in a hopeful manner." Many men kiss in that
manner, but what the writer probably meant was, "I
hope he will kiss me." When it comes to kissing, it is
best to say what you mean.

Faulty: Hopefully it will not rain on
         Thanksgiving.

Better: I hope that it will not rain on
         Thanksgiving.

18. **OVERUSE OF "VERY."** Immature writers
sometimes overuse the adverb "very" as an
intensifier. More mature writers discover that they
can improve most pieces of writing by eliminating

nine "very's" out of ten. Often the word being intensified by "very" can be replaced by a more powerful word.

Faulty: It was very hot the day Michael took his very difficult achievement tests, and he is very sure that he would have been accepted by a very much better college if it had been cooler that day.

Better: It was sweltering the day Michael took his achievement tests. He is sure that if it had been cooler that day he would have been accepted by a more respected college.

19. **MISUSE OF "LIE" AND "LAY."** Most writers know that "to lie" can have different meanings. It can mean, for example, "to tell a fib," but it can also mean "to rest horizontally." They sometimes, however, confuse "to lie" with "to lay," which usually means "to place a thing on a flat surface." The confusion is caused partly by the fact that the word "lay" can be both the present tense of "lay" and the past tense of "lie." The sentences "John decided to lie down on the couch" and "John lay down on the couch" both refer to John's resting horizontally. Both are correct. For some writers the confusion comes when they forget that present and past forms of "lie" ("lay," "lain") require no direct object, whereas the present and past forms of "lay" ("laid," "laid") do require a direct object.

Faulty: Billy laid flat on the table.

Early this morning, Mary said, she lay the only copy of her paper on the table.

Better: Billy lay flat on the table.

Early this morning, Mary said, she laid the only copy of her paper on the table.

20. SPLIT INFINITIVE. An infinitive is said to be "split" when a modifier comes between "to" and the base verb form. Although the split infinitive is gradually becoming more common and more acceptable, you are usually well advised to avoid it in formal writing. To correct a split infinitive, move the modifier.

Faulty: The students planned to carefully prepare for the quiz.

Better: The students planned to prepare carefully for the quiz.

21. MISMATCHED PARALLEL ELEMENTS. Faulty parallelism occurs when the items listed in a sentence do not follow a common or parallel structural or grammatical pattern. Your writing will be clearer and more emphatic if you put such items in parallel form.

Faulty: My busy life at school includes choir, acting in plays, and bike riding.

> ***Better:*** My busy life at school includes
> singing in the choir, acting in
> college plays, and riding my bike.

22. CONFUSION OF COMPARATIVE AND SUPERLATIVE FORMS. Most adjectives and adverbs have what are called comparative forms ("older," "bolder," "better," "more relaxed," "more frequently"), used when comparing two items. They also have superlative forms ("oldest," "boldest," "best," "most relaxed," "most frequently"), used when comparing more than two items. Typically, use "-er" and "-est" forms for one-syllable and some two-syllable adjectives and adverbs. Typically, use "more" and "most" for some two-syllable and all three-syllable adjectives and adverbs. For two-syllable words, you sometimes have a choice: either "funnier" and "funniest" or "more funny" and "most funny." Common practice will often be our best guide. Do not, however, confuse superlatives with comparatives, and do not double-compare. Shakespeare in *Julius Caesar* could get away with having one of his characters refer to "the most unkindest cut of all," but you're not Shakespeare.

> ***Faulty:*** Which tastes best to you, butter or
> margarine?
>
> Of the five presidents I have worked
> under, Timothy McConnell was both
> the more kinder and demandinger.
>
> Sally is more young than Anne.
>
> Tim is charminger than Paul.

Better: Which tastes better to you, butter
       or margarine?

       Of the five presidents I have worked
       under, Timothy McConnell was both
       the kindest and the most demanding.

       Sally is younger than Anne.

       Tim is more charming than Paul.

Words such as "unique," "ultimate," "primary," and
so on, cannot be intensified by adding "very" or
compared by adding "less," "least," "more," "most,"
or some other similar adjective.

Faulty: Greg's highest ultimate goal was to
        design an extremely unique battery-
        powered skateboard.

Better: Greg's ultimate goal was to design a
        unique battery-powered skateboard.

23. **WORDINESS.** Many people tend to think that
    more is better. The more money they earn, the more
    successful they are. The more lovers they have, the
    better their emotional life. And the more words
    they use, the better their writing. As they mature
    they see the fallacy of such assumptions. Certainly
    wordiness is one of the sins beginning writers must
    quickly learn to avoid.

    Faulty: There is evidence that many males
            of all ages are given to a certain
            questioning of their traditional
            beliefs in what is good, and indeed
            even that they question whether
            there is any good at all in the

world. These men may not make a lot
of commotion about their despairing
feelings, but they have those
feelings nevertheless, most of the
time.

Better: The mass of men lead lives of quiet
desperation.

24. **REDUNDANCY.** Another form of wordiness that
sometimes traps writers is needless repetition. In
the first example, note that emotions are feelings,
and that a murder cannot be other than fatal:

Faulty: He had emotional feelings when
his English teacher was fatally
murdered.

Hamlet seems confused, uncertain,
and puzzled.

Better: He was deeply disturbed when his
English teacher was murdered.

Throughout the play Hamlet seems
confused.

25. **CLICHÉS.** Good writers strive to keep freshness
in their writing by avoiding expressions that have
become hackneyed or overused: "tried and true," "a
slow burn," "you better believe it," "deader than a
doornail," "a done deal," "pro-active," "hands-on,"
"state-of-the-art," "shovel-ready," "interface," "it's
not rocket science," "at the end of the day," "at this
point in time," "24/7," "with all due respect." There
is no foolproof way to avoid clichés, but do strive for
freshness in your expressions.

Faulty: We must get together soon to
interface about the statewide
impact of the new legislation.

We worked 24/7 to put together a
pro-active contract, but at the end
of the day the union, with all due
respect, deep-sixed it.

Better: We must get together soon to
discuss the impact of the new
legislation all across Oregon.

We spent all week on what we hoped
was a contract the union would
accept, but the members turned it
down.

26. OMITTED TRANSITIONS.
Transitions are links that tell readers of the connection between ideas. Transitions should be used both to connect ideas within a paragraph and to link the idea in one paragraph to an idea in the next paragraph.

Faulty: Steve was a brilliant quarterback.
He often performed erratically.

Better: Although Steve was a brilliant
quarterback, he often performed
erratically.

Steve was a brilliant quarterback,
yet he often performed erratically.

Transitions between paragraphs, of course, are usually longer and more informative and often refer back to the previous point as well as look forward to the next one: "In addition to Dean Cooper's directing us to report any stealing we saw, he also emphasized that we should help the police maintain safety by walking in pairs around campus late at night." It is best to place your transitions at the start of the new paragraph rather than at the end of the previous one. Much of the writing that you do in the professional world must be "skimmable." Most of your readers will be busy businesspeople who will have the time only to skim your work. As they do so they may be looking for quite specific information or opinions. You can make it easier for them to find what they are looking for if you get into the habit of placing the transitions at the start of each paragraph or section.

Here is a list of some transitional devices that can help show the relationships among your ideas and make your sentences and paragraphs flow smoothly from beginning to end:

admittedly	in addition	of course
although	in conclusion	on the contrary
as a result	indeed	on the other hand
assuredly	in fact	still
but	in other words	the fact remains
certainly	it is true that	therefore
clearly, then	likewise	thus
consequently	moreover	to be sure
even so	nevertheless	true
for example	nobody denies	undoubtedly
furthermore	no doubt	unquestionably
granted	obviously	yet

27. MISSPELLED WORDS. Although there is disagreement about how important spelling really is to good writing, no one doubts that sloppy spelling is distracting. It always draws attention to itself, and when it does so it takes your reader's attention, if only for a second, off what you are saying. Here is a list of words that college students most frequently misspell:

a lot
absence
accept, except
accommodate
achievement
acquire
across
advice, advise
affect, effect
alleged
all right
allude, elude
always, all ways
argument
basically
believable
benefited
capital, capitol
captain
category
colonel
commitment
committed
comparative
compliment,
    complement

comprised
conceivable
conscientious
criticize
curiosity
deceive
definite
despair,
    desperate
desert, dessert
develop
disastrous
discreet, discrete
divine
elicit, illicit
embarrass
environment
erroneous
exaggerate
existence
farther, further
fascinate
February
forty
friend
grammar

hypocrisy
immigrate,
    emigrate
inflammable
interrupt
irresistible
its, it's
loneliness
loose, lose
maneuver
miscellaneous
misspell
moral, morale
occurrence
parallel
pastime
precede
prejudice
principal,
    principle
proceed,
    procedure
professor
publicly
questionnaire
quiet, quite

receive	skiing	unnecessary
recommend	stationary,	until
remembrance	stationery	vacuum
repetition	succeed	vengeance
rhythm	than, then	villain
roommate	their, there,	weather,
ridiculous	they're	whether
seize	tries	weird
separate	truly	whose, who's
sergeant	twelfth	your, you're

28. REPETITIOUS SENTENCE PATTERNS.

Some writers fall into the standard subject-verb sentence pattern. You can enliven your writing by experimenting with other patterns.

Faulty: I went to town. I wanted to buy a pound of chopped beef. I found just what I was looking for at Smith's Supermarket. I bought it. I found out when I got home that it was actually chopped lamb. I hate lamb, so I threw it away. I realize now that I should have taken it back and exchanged it.

Better: Wanting to buy a pound of chopped beef, I walked to Smith's Supermarket. When I got home with my packet and found out it was chopped lamb, I threw it into the garbage because I hate lamb. That was silly of me. The store would have exchanged it.

Especially when writing on a computer, it is easy to build long sentences by plopping in an "and" and

just writing on and on. That is often a good strategy
for getting your ideas down quickly, but you will
want to revise by combining the clauses in different
ways or just breaking the long sentences into shorter
ones.

Faulty: Huckleberry Finn was afraid of
his father, and he was eager to
escape the cabin and run off down
the river. He chanced to run into
Jim and discovered that they both
were slaves and so they made their
escape together.

Better: Afraid of his father, Huckleberry
Finn escaped the cabin. When he
stumbled upon the runaway slave Jim
and realized that they were both
escaped slaves, Huck decided to run
down the river with him.

It is good to be aware that there are a number of
ways to say essentially the same thing. Good stylists
consider alternative phrasing as they revise their
work, if only to shift the tone of their writing.

Acceptable: I like to use chopsticks when
I eat in a Chinese restaurant,
even though I do not use them
skillfully.

Alternatives: Even though I always drop
bits of food, when I eat in a
Chinese restaurant I like to use
chopsticks.

Chopsticks are my preference when I
eat in a Chinese restaurant, but I

am a slow learner and I drop some
of my food.

Brave but sloppy, I always ask for
chopsticks in a Chinese restaurant.

The waitress at the Three Dragons
knows that I expect her to bring
me chopsticks. She never complains
about the mess I make.

29. FAULTY PRESENTATION OF NUMBERS.
Generally, the numbers up to a hundred should
be spelled out—"six" rather than "6"—unless you
are giving page numbers, referring to dates, or
making mathematical references. Round numbers—
hundreds, thousands, hundred thousands, and
millions—are usually spelled out (except in the
sciences). If a big number comes at the start of a
sentence, spell it out or recast the sentence:

Faulty: 520 cows and 4 bulls died in the
flood of nineteen hundred.

The city's population is more than
100,000.

Better: Five hundred twenty cows and four
bulls died in the flood of 1900.

In the flood of 1900 we lost 520
cows and four bulls.

The city's population is more than
one hundred thousand.

30. OMITTED COMMA.
One of the most annoying
little devils in writing is the common comma.
Commas are used for all sorts of purposes, like

indicating a pause, showing a grammatical function, or separating items otherwise confused. Often there is no "right" and "wrong" with commas—just good judgment. Students sometimes omit commas when they should put them in. After long introductory phrases, for example, it is usually better to put in a comma.

Faulty: At most of the other college
        campuses with which I am familiar
        no wall separates the campus from
        the surrounding community.

Better: At most of the other college
        campuses with which I am familiar,
        no wall separates the campus from
        the surrounding community.

After shorter introductory phrases, no comma is usually needed: "At King's College no wall separates the campus from the surrounding community."

    A second commonly omitted comma is the final comma setting off items in a series. Although newspaper writers eager to save space leave off the final comma in a series, the result is sometimes confusing. Most professional writers, more concerned with meaning than with space, leave it in. In the faulty example here, it is not clear whether Mary likes strawberry ice cream *with* pickles or both strawberry ice cream and pickles.

Faulty: Mary likes chocolate pie, chicken
        nuggets, iced tea, liver and
        onions, strawberry ice cream and
        pickles.

Better: Mary likes chocolate pie, chicken
         nuggets, iced tea, liver and
         onions, strawberry ice cream, and
         pickles.

A third commonly omitted comma involves
what are sometimes called nonrestrictive
elements. A nonrestrictive element adds
information not necessary to the identification
of the person or term it modifies. When we say
"Mr. Wallace is a man who really knows how to
teach," the who-clause is said to be restrictive
because it identifies who or what Mr. Wallace is.
When we say, "Mr. Wallace, who really knows
how to teach, won a major teaching award last
year," the who-clause is said to be nonrestrictive
because it merely adds information not essential
to the sentence. Nonrestrictive clauses are set off
by commas.

Faulty: The yellow cat which had only one
         front paw was our most successful
         mouser.

Better: The yellow cat, which had only
         one paw, was our most successful
         mouser.

In these sentences there is only one yellow
cat and that cat also happens to have only one
front paw. If there are several yellow cats, only
one of which has a front paw missing, you might
want to rephrase the sentence to make the
element restrictive: "Our most successful mouser

was the yellow cat with only one front paw." In that sentence the restrictive element needs no comma because it is essential that we distinguish the one-pawed yellow cat from other yellow cats.

A fourth common omission of the comma is found in sentences involving words like "too" (meaning "also"), "however," and "therefore." These words are usually set off by a pair of commas.

Faulty: Thomas too, was sickly as a child.

Shakespeare however, wrote sonnets to his "dark lady."

Better: Thomas, too, was sickly as a child.

Shakespeare, however, wrote sonnets to his "dark lady."

A fifth common omission of the comma occurs in sentences made up of two independent clauses. If a two-clause sentence names two separate subjects or mentions the same subject twice, you should usually place a comma before the conjunction.

Faulty: Tom rode his motorcycle nearly five hundred miles to Junction and the reporters all interviewed the new mayor.

We get only one chance to live on this earth and we might as well make the best of the experience.

Better: Tom rode his motorcycle nearly five hundred miles to Junction, and the

```
reporters all interviewed the new
mayor.
```

```
We get only one chance to live on
this earth, and we might as well
make the best of the experience.
```

One way to remember this rule is that the comma
helps us to avoid reading the beginning of the second
clause as a possible compound predicate: "Tom rode
his motorcycle to Junction and the reporters." If
the second element is not a clause—that is, has no
subject of its own—then no comma is needed: "Tom
rode his motorcycle to Junction and interviewed the
mayor." With short clauses, or where no confusion
is possible, good writers sometimes eliminate the
comma even though they repeat the subject: "He
came to Junction and he conquered my heart."

   A sixth kind of omitted comma is one needed
to separate coordinate adjectives—two or more
adjectives that can be joined by "and"—that each
modify a noun separately. Note that if the adjectives
are cumulative and do not separately modify the
noun, no comma is necessary. One test is whethere
it makes sense to add an "and" before the last
adjective.

Faulty: Tom has an incurable chronic
          progressive disease of the brain
          that will one day require that he
          be placed in a nursing home.

          I own two, big, white pickup
          trucks.

Better: Tom has an incurable, chronic,
progressive disease of the brain
that will one day require that he
be placed in a nursing home.

I own two big white pickup trucks.

Note that you might say "incurable and chronic
and progressive disease," but not "two and big and
white pickup trucks."

A seventh kind of omitted comma is one used to
head off an unfortunate misinterpretation. In the
following sentences, it sounds at first as if Stan is
a passenger in the car and as if the campers are
eating a wild dog.

Faulty: If you drive Stan will take the
train.

As we were sitting around the
campfire eating a wild dog barked a
short distance off to the west.

Better: If you drive, Stan will take the
train.

As we were sitting around the
campfire eating, a wild dog barked
a short distance off to the west.

31. **UNNECESSARY COMMA.** Some writers tend to
stick a comma wherever they sense a natural pause
in the sentence. Current practice is generally to use
commas sparingly.

Faulty: Fred was not sure, if he should
meet Sally at the station, or
at the restaurant where they,
frequently, met.

My book, *Risk Teaching*, brings
together some of my essays on
pedagogy.

Recycling your old newspapers is
better, than burning them in an
incinerator.

Are you coming to see me?," she
asked.

Better: Fred was not sure if he should meet
Sally at the station or at the
restaurant where they frequently
met.

My book *Risk Teaching* brings
together some of my essays on
pedagogy.

Recycling your old newspapers is
better than burning them in an
incinerator.

"Are you coming to see me?" she
asked.

32. OVERUSED EXCLAMATION POINT. Beginning
writers often tend to use too many exclamation
points to give emphasis to their statements. You can
get through this whole course without using any of
these marks! Give emphasis in other ways, such as
through the use of stronger, more vivid verbs.

Faulty: Mary went quickly to town on her
horse, weeping all the way!

Better: Mary galloped to town, her eyes
streaming with tears.

33. **MISUSED SEMICOLON.** Many good writers
    almost never use semicolons. If you must use them,
    remember that a semicolon usually functions as
    a weak period, not as a strong comma. That is,
    you use it where you would normally use a period,
    not where you would normally use a comma.
    Sometimes you can use it in place of a period
    between independent clauses if you want to show a
    close relationship or a special balance between the
    two clauses. A semicolon can also be used before
    conjunctive adverbs such as "however," "therefore,"
    and "thus," but usually not before coordinating
    conjunctions such as "and" and "but."

    Faulty: The experiment had failed; and
              therefore testing began again.

    Better: The experiment had failed;
              therefore testing began again.

              The experiment had failed, but
              testing began again.

    Because there are usually attractive alternatives to
    the semicolon, use it only if nothing else will do the
    job more simply.

34. **OMITTED COLON.** Used correctly, a colon follows
    a complete statement and introduces a clarifying
    restatement, a list of items, or a block quotation. To
    test for correct colon usage, see if you can logically
    insert the word "namely" after the colon.

Faulty: The college offered: a new scholarship. Full tuition plus the cost of books.

Better: The college offered a new scholarship: full tuition plus the cost of books.

The college offered a new scholarship with full tuition and books.

35. MISUSED DASH. A dash is often used to show an interruption in thought within a sentence or to add explanatory material. Unlike parentheses (which deemphasize the material added) dashes call attention to the interrupting material. Be sure that the sentence would be coherent if the portion within the dashes were omitted.

Faulty: The dorm looked like a disaster area—laundry piled on the bed, books scattered on the floor—and McDonald's wrappers stuffed in the closet.

His car shiny and red—attracted a lot of attention.

Better: The dorm looked like a disaster area—laundry piled on the bed, books scattered on the floor, and McDonald's wrappers stuffed in the closet.

His car—shiny and red—attracted a lot of attention.

36. OMITTED HYPHEN. You should usually use a hyphen to join a compound modifier that precedes a noun.

Faulty: `The chocolate covered cake was`
`delicious.`

`The Beatles began a major trend in`
`twentieth century music.`

Better: `The chocolate-covered cake was`
`delicious.`

`The Beatles began a major trend in`
`twentieth-century music.`

Note that these words are not hyphenated in other contexts: "We live in the twentieth century." And note that some commonly associated words need not be hyphenated, even before a noun: "These Girl Scout cookies taste stale."

The hyphen is sometimes used in compound nouns or verbs: "secretary-treasurer," "president-elect," "father-figure," and "water-ski" (used as a verb only; the noun is "water ski"). Because fashions change on hyphenating such compounds—the verb "skydive" was once "sky-dive" and the noun "high school" was once "highschool"—it is best to consult a recent dictionary for any words you are not sure of.

37. MISUSED PARENTHESES. Parentheses are used to enclose explanatory material such as an illustration, a side comment, or a citation. Unlike

the dash, parentheses tell the reader that the added
material is of secondary importance. Be sure to
punctuate the rest of the sentence as if the material
in the parentheses did not exist. Avoid overuse of
parentheses, especially when the enclosed material
would be more effective in a separate sentence.

Faulty: The river was dark (where had the
day gone?) when we approached the
dock.

Better: The river was dark when we
approached the dock. Where had the
day gone?

38. MISUSED SQUARE BRACKETS. Use square
brackets to indicate that you are adding explanatory
words to a quoted passage. Most authors now
consider it acceptable to alter, without brackets,
the capitalization of the first word in a quotation
and the use of commas and periods at the end of a
quotation.

Faulty: Hawthorne says, "[h]e stole forward
until the light glared full upon
his (Brown's) eyes[,]" but he does
not indicate why that light is
important.

Better: Hawthorne says, "he stole forward
until the light glared full upon
his [Brown's] eyes," but he does
not indicate why that light is
important.

Sometimes square brackets are used inside
parentheses to avoid the need for confusing double
parentheses.

Faulty: He is said to speak in a "hoarse
whisper" (327 (376 in the Oxford
edition)).

Better: He is said to speak in a "hoarse
whisper" (327 [376 in the Oxford
edition]).

39. MISUSED POSSESSIVE FORMS. The
apostrophe serves a number of functions. The
possessive form of a noun is indicated by an
apostrophe. Most errors involve the failure to
use the apostrophe to indicate possession. To
test whether you have a possessive noun, try
substituting an "of (noun)" construction.

Faulty: My roommates stereo [the stereo of
my roommate] was playing at full
volume.

A persons right [the right of a
person] to privacy is violated in
college.

Better: My roommate's stereo was playing
at full volume.

A person's right to privacy is
violated in college.

Because inanimate objects cannot really "own"
things, most experienced writers use an "of" phrase

rather than possessive case to assign properties to such objects.

Faulty: The tree's leaves were green.

Better: The leaves of the tree were green.

To make most plural nouns possessive add an apostrophe after the final "s."

Faulty: I returned the students essays at the end of class.

Better: I returned the students' essays at the end of class.

The possessive case of pronouns does not require an apostrophe: "hers," not "her's." You should keep in mind two facts. First, the possessive pronoun "its" requires no apostrophe and should not be confused with "it's," which is the contraction for "it is." Second, the noun "one" is not a pronoun and so requires the apostrophe to show possession.

Faulty: The cat licked it's paw.

Ones honor is all that really matters.

Better: The cat licked its paw.

One's honor is all that really matters.

The possessive case is still usually used with a gerund—a noun made from a verb and ending in

"-ing." The modifying subject of a gerund usually needs to be in the possessive case.

Faulty: Sam making the forty-foot putt was a surprise.

They laughed at Julia wearing her hat backward.

Better: Sam's making the forty-foot putt was a surprise.

They laughed at Julia's wearing her hat backward.

40. OVERUSED CONTRACTIONS. In addition to being used to show possession, an apostrophe is used to join two words in a contraction—an abbreviated joining of two words—to replace the omitted letter or letters. In formal writing it is usually best to avoid most contractions. Your readers may in effect contract the words as they read them, but it is quite all right for you to spell out the full forms.

Faulty: The mayor didn't listen to Tom's request because he thought politicians wouldn't win votes by listening to environmentalists.

Better: The mayor did not listen to Tom's request because he thought politicians would not win votes by listening to environmentalists.

Of course, it is not wrong to use contractions, even in the formal writing you do in college, but overuse of contractions can make your essays sound distractingly chatty. My own practice is to use the full form unless I am quoting direct speech.

41. **MISSPELLED CONTRACTIONS.** A common spelling mistake may occur when you form a contraction using a conditional verb form ("would," "could," "may," "might") with "have." Do not be fooled by the way the contracted word sounds ("could've," "might've"):

Faulty: I could of danced all night.

You might of passed the test if you had studied.

Better: I could have danced all night.

You might have passed the test if you had studied.

42. **OMITTED QUOTATION MARKS.** When you are writing about a published essay or work of literature, you may want to quote from it as you explain or support your own ideas. When you do quote more than a word or two from a source, use quotation marks.

Faulty: Hawthorne says that Young Goodman Brown stole forward until the light glared full upon his eyes.

Better: Hawthorne says that Young Goodman Brown "stole forward until the light glared full upon his eyes" (724).

Note that when you are punctuating the end of
a quotation, the comma and period go after the
closing parenthesis even if they had been in the
quotation. The exclamation point and question
mark go inside the quotation mark if they were part
of the quotation. Note, too, that if an exclamation
point or question mark is part of the quotation, then
the sentence also requires a period following the
reference.

Faulty: The king says angrily to Sir
Blanchard, "Go, on pain of death,
and come back no more"! (322). A
month later, however, Blanchard
returns and says humbly to the
king, "My lord, I have brought news
of your daughter." (336)

Better: The king says angrily to Sir
Blanchard, "Go, on pain of death,
and come back no more!" (332). A
month later, however, Blanchard
returns and says humbly to the
king, "My lord, I have brought news
of your daughter" (336).

These examples apply to shorter quotations run in
with your own sentences. With block quotations the
parenthetical page number stands by itself outside
the final punctuation of the quoted passage. **See 45,
BLOCK QUOTATIONS**, for an example.

43. **MISUSED ELLIPSES.** When you leave out part
of a quotation, indicate the omission with ellipses,
or double-spaced periods. If you omit part of a

sentence, use three such periods. If you leave out
a sentence or more, use four periods. Most authors
leave off the ellipses at the start and the end of a
quotation, it being understood that of course there
was something before and something after.

Faulty: Hawthorne says, ". . . he stole
forward until the light glared full
upon his eyes."

Better: Hawthorne says, "he stole forward
until the light glared full upon
his eyes."

44. **REGULAR QUOTATIONS.** When you quote
material, you should indicate the source. A common
convention when you are quoting from an essay
or a work of literature from an assigned college
text is to give the page numbers in parentheses.
Your teacher and your classmates will assume
that the text is your source and will not demand
that you footnote all of your quotations. When you
quote something, normally put the page number in
parentheses outside the quotation mark but before
the punctuation, unless a "?" or "!" is part of the
quotation.

Faulty: "Call me Ishmael," (12) the
narrator tells us. Then he tells us
more about himself: "When I go to
sea, I go as a simple sailor." (14)

In Melville's *Moby-Dick* an English
sailor says, "Blood! but that old
man's a grand old cove! We are the

```
       lads to hunt him up his whale"
       (153)!
```

Better: `"Call me Ishmael" (12), the`
`narrator tells us. Then he tells us`
`more about himself: "When I go to`
`sea, I go as a simple sailor" (14).`

`In Melville's Moby-Dick an English`
`sailor says, "Blood! but that old`
`man's a grand old cove! We are the`
`lads to hunt him  up his whale!"`
`(153).`

When you are quoting fewer than three full lines of
poetry, run the lines into your own sentences, use
quotation marks, indicate line ends with a virgule,
or slash mark, and indicate the page or line numbers
in parentheses. Here is an example:

```
The old man in Chaucer's Pardoner's
Tale says that because he cannot find
someone to exchange his youth for
the old man's age, he must keep his
"old age stille / As longe tyme as
it is Goddes wille" (VI 725-26).
```

When you are quoting three or more lines of poetry
or longer chunks of prose, set the lines off as a
separate block, indented, and put the page or line
numbers outside the final punctuation. **See next
item, 45, BLOCK QUOTATIONS**, for an example.

45. **BLOCK QUOTATIONS.** When quoting a passage
of three or more lines of poetry or six or more lines
of prose, use block quotation form. To block-quote,

simply indent the quoted material five spaces or
one tab in from the left margin. Your instructor
will probably want you to single-space indented
block quotations. Most publishers, however, insist
on double spacing of all material submitted for
publication. No quotation marks are necessary
unless there is quoted material, such as dialogue, in
the quotation. Always introduce the quotation with
your own words, and always connect the quotation
with your own sentence, at least with a colon. Here
is an example:

> Young Goodman Brown reacts violently
> when his wife is led forward to the
> strange red-glowing rock. He hears
> many strange noises and voices:
>> The cry of grief, rage, and terror
>> was yet piercing the night, when
>> the unhappy husband held his
>> breath for a response. There was
>> a scream, drowned immediately in
>> a loud murmur of voices, fading
>> into far-off laughter, as the dark
>> cloud swept away, leaving the
>> clear and silent sky above Goodman
>> Brown. (258)
>
> What do these cries, screams,
> murmuring voices, and laughter
> represent? We cannot, of course, be
> sure, because Hawthorne leaves his
> meaning ambiguous. Still, we wonder
> if these sounds are Young Goodman
> Brown's own crazy babblings, the
> babblings of a man caught up in the
> frenzy of diabolism.

Notice not only the placement of the page number but also that the writer has connected the quotation to his preceding sentence and commented on it afterward. Too many beginning writers plop in disconnected quotations and neglect to interpret them.

To discourage padding an essay with unnecessary quotations, most teachers ask that you ignore block quotations in your word or page count. Thus, a "three-page essay" means three pages of your words, not two of yours and one of block quotations.

46. **TITLE.** Always provide a fitting and engaging title for your essay. Do not merely repeat the topic you were given. Rather, select a title that fits not merely the topic the teacher assigned, but the particular essay that you wrote. Ideally, of course, your title should be an inviting first step toward your thesis.

> Topic: Problems with parking at OSU
>
> Title: **Parking Chaos on Eighth Street**

Capitalize the important words in the title. Unless an article, coordinating conjunction, or preposition appears as the first or last word in a title, leave it lower case. It is a good idea to center and use boldface type for your title, or in some other way (italics or larger type size) distinguish it from the rest of your essay.

47. LACK OF CARING. The best writers find ways of showing that they care about their writing. They write in such a way that they both interest and persuade their readers. They show commitment to their ideas. They revise and edit attentively and make their final drafts neat. The best writers, aware that essays have voices of their own, turn in essays that say, almost reverentially, "My creator cares about me."

INDEX

QUICK REFERENCE GUIDE
TO *EDITING MATTERS*

1. Fragment
2. Comma splice
3. Fused sentences
4. Tense shift
5. Faulty subject-verb agreement
6. Faulty pronoun-antecedent agreement
7. Ambiguous pronoun reference
8. Shift in person
9. Dangling modifiers
10. Passive voice
11. Sexist language
12. Careless use of "you"
13. Vague use of "this"
14. Misuse of "who" and "whom"
15. Misuse of "which" and "that"
16. Misuse of "however"
17. Misuse of "hopefully"
18. Overuse of "very"
19. Misuse of "lie" and "lay"
20. Split infinitive
21. Mismatched parallel elements
22. Confusion of comparative and superlative forms
23. Wordiness
24. Redundancy
25. Clichés
26. Omitted transitions
27. Misspelled words
28. Repetitious sentence patterns
29. Faulty presentation of numbers
30. Omitted comma
31. Unnecessary comma
32. Overused exclamation point
33. Misused semicolon
34. Omitted colon
35. Misused dash
36. Omitted hyphen
37. Misused parentheses
38. Misused square brackets
39. Misused possessive forms
40. Overused contractions
41. Misspelled contractions
42. Omitted quotation marks
43. Misused ellipses
44. Regular quotations
45. Block quotations
46. Title
47. Lack of caring

PROOFREADER'S MARKS

Perhaps your teacher will use the following proofreader's marks
in the margins of your essay as a kind of shorthand to indicate
editing you should do.

℘	= delete
∧	= insert
#	= add space
◡	= close up space
⊙	= period
⋏	= comma
⋎	= apostrophe
⋎⋎	= quotation marks
∽	= transpose
sp	= spell out
stet	= no correction; let it stand
/	= (through letter) change to lower case
≡	= (placed under letter) change to upper case
¶	= start a new paragraph here
no ¶	= no new paragraph here

Made in the USA
Middletown, DE
09 January 2018